The Home-Based Business Kit

From Hobby to Profit

Diana Brodman Summers
D-M Boulay
Attorneys at Law

SPHINX® PUBLISHING
AN IMPRINT OF SOURCEBOOKS, INC.®
NAPERVILLE, ILLINOIS
www.SphinxLegal.com

Copyright © 2005 by Diana Brodman Summers and D-M Boulay
Cover and internal design © 2005 by Sourcebooks, Inc.

First Edition: 2005

This publication is designed to provide accurate and authoritative information in regard to the subject matter covered. It is sold with the understanding that the publisher is not engaged in rendering legal, accounting, or other professional service. If legal advice or other expert assistance is required, the services of a competent professional person should be sought.
　　—From a Declaration of Principles Jointly Adopted by a Committee of the American
　　　Bar Association and a Committee of Publishers and Associations

Published by Sourcebooks, Inc.
P.O. Box 4410, Naperville, Illinois 60567-4410
(630) 961-3900
Fax: (630) 961-2168
www.sourcebooks.com

Library of Congress Cataloging-in-Publication Data

Summers, Diana Brodman.
  The home-based business kit / by Diana Brodman Summers and D-M Boulay
      p. cm.
  ISBN-13: 978-1-57248-484-9 (pbk. : alk. paper)
  ISBN-10: 1-57248-484-5 (pbk. : alk. paper)
 1. Home-based businesses--Management. 2. New business
enterprises--Management. I. Title.

HD62.38.S86 2005
658.1'1412--dc22

2005021729

Printed and bound in the United States of America
BG   10 9 8 7 6 5 4 3 2 1

Contents

Section I: Evaluate Your Home for Business

Section II: Start Getting Organized

Your Time is Valuable
Choose a Business You Can Grow to Love
Identify Your Goals
Create a Daily Activity List
Analyze Your Activity List
Focus Your Initiative
Identify Your Business Skills
Know Your Personal Limitations
Develop Balance in Your Life

Prioritize Your Tasks
Plan Your Time
Too Much Work and Not Enough Time
Control Your Interruptions
Project Scheduling Challenges
Inventory Scheduling Challenges

Section III: Develop Your Plans

Start-Up Action Plan
The Importance of a Business Plan
Developing a Business Plan
Writing a Business Plan
Presenting Your Business Plan
Putting Your Business Plan to Work
Sample Business Plan

Determine the Marketability
Learn About the Competition
Spot Trends
Think Outside the Box
Write a Marketing Plan
Home-Based Business Marketing Plan
Truth in Advertising
Implementing Your Marketing Plan

Section IV: Put Your Plan into Action

Introduction

This book is a culmination of the experiences of many people. Both authors are small business owners who began with home-based businesses. Additionally, we have assisted many clients, friends, and family members in starting their own home businesses.

For us the enjoyment has been watching a business grow from the first glimmer of an idea to a money-making career. The purpose of this book is to assist the readers from the initial thought of wanting to start a home-based business, to deciding what business to start, to getting you and your family prepared.

We begin with our *10 Steps to Success*. This short section identifies concepts and actions that you can consider right now. Then, we begin to help you make the decision to start a business by discussing the common reasons people start home-based businesses. Once you have made the decision to work from home, it is time to discuss the variety of businesses that easily fit in a home based environment. We look at how you can accentuate the positives and reduce the negatives in each type of home-based business. If you do not know what type of business you could be good at, there are checklists and questionnaires to help determine your personal talents.

Following the discussion of the types of businesses, you must determine if your home is the right place for that business. We discuss it all—laws, neighbors, naysayers, and your family. Steps are even suggested to keep your family and your property safe while operating a business from your home.

Once you have decided on the type of business you want to locate in your home, this book helps you set both business and personal goals. We provide information on how to set short-term and long-term goals that you can easily track to see how the business is doing. We give you the tools to organize your business ideas so you can clearly develop a business and easily measure the progress of that business. There are also tips on how to prioritize your business duties, and we provide time-saving ideas, so you can use your time wisely. In addition, we give the reader tools on how to remain flexible in the direction of their business so that each success and each failure can be quickly evaluated, resolved, and used for the growth of the business.

This book assists the home-based business owner in developing a business plan that can be used in presentations for loans and for community events. It also helps you decide how to market your home-based business. In addition, it will help you to make a budget or financial plan for the business.

Another section in the book gives you steps you need to actually start-up your home-based business. We discuss the legal considerations of selecting a business form, including the positives and negatives of each type of business structure and what it means to you and your family. We also discuss how to deal with others in your business such as lawyers, accountants, insurance agents, and other business experts.

Finally, this book helps you run your home-based business on a day-to-day basis. We give you information on how to deal with customers, how to get customers to pay your bills, and how to set a fair customer policy. We then discuss dealing with vendors, how to research a vendor, and what to do when a vendor lets you down. In addition, for the future growth of your business, we give you information on dealing with employees, both from a legal and personal side.

If you have ever thought of opening a home-based business, this book will give you a taste of what setting up and running a business is like without ever getting out of your easy chair. If you are planning to open a home-based business, this book will give you ideas, checklists, case studies, and places to go for even more information. Whether you are just thinking about starting a home-based business or are actively planning to start one now, this book is for you.

10 Steps to Making
Your Home-Based Business
a Success

You have a great idea for a home-based business. In fact, you are spending considerable time thinking about your future business and can't wait to get started. Here are ten steps you can take right now, that will help to make your home-based business a success.

1. Involve your family in planning your home-based business.

Remember, your business will be running out of the family home, so include your family in the business at the very beginning. Older family members can help you stake out that separate area in the house that is just for your business. They may also be able to do some minor work for your business. The younger ones may be able to support your business by taking on more chores or just by being quiet when Mommy or Daddy is on a business call.

Use your family members as your first *focus group* to discuss your product. Ask their opinions. Would they buy the product? How would they change/improve the product?

Get the entire family involved and excited about your home-based business—their love and support will make your life easier.

2. Set aside a certain space just for your business.

A home-based business needs a location, even in the smallest of homes. You need a place that is set aside to keep all your business documents and, depending on your business, the products you are working on. You will also need space to store the products made before sale (inventory) and to store the parts that go into making your product (ingredients, components).

Home-based businesses can run from the corner of a room, in a rebuilt closet, from an extra bedroom, from the basement, from the garage, or even out of a small file cabinet. The only requirement is that you keep all your business materials in one place and not spread throughout the house where they can be misplaced or lost.

3. Get all the preliminary work done before you open your business.

Every business, even one that is home-based, must do some preliminary things in order to become a real business. This may mean registering your business in your state, getting financial accounts set up, and finding someone to supply you with the raw materials to make your first product. Your home-based business may need to have a computer in place, an additional phone line brought into your home, commercial cooking pans, or just printed business cards. Make sure all these preliminary tasks are completed before you open your business so you are able to hit the ground running on your first day of being a business owner.

4. Keep expenses low to start.

You probably cannot start up a home-based business on a dime, but you can pinch pennies on start-up costs. Make a list of what you need to start your business. Now go over that list and prioritize that spending. See if you can get by with smaller quantities, postpone a purchase, or use something you already have on hand. By keeping the start-up expenses low, you can concentrate on selling your product because it is a good product, not just selling to pay the bills.

5. Know what you are selling.

This is your business, and you need to know everything about what you sell whether it is a product or a service. If you are making a product, you should be familiar with everything that goes into your product, such as components and ingredients, exactly how it is made, how long it takes to assemble or cook, etc. You will be looked at as the expert, so make sure that you have the answers or know where to find them.

6. Treat all your customers with respect, even when they don't buy anything.

Be kind to your customers, even when they are having bad days. Often a calm voice and a kind word can do more to get you a sale than advertising. Answer the customer's questions, offer assistance, and be ready to give the customer a refund if your product fails.

7. Sell your products or services for a fair price.

Along with treating your customers with respect, make sure you set a fair price for your product or service. If you set your prices too high, you can scare off good customers. On the other hand, if you price too low, the customers may feel that they are getting inferior work. Your prices should reflect the cost to produce the item or service, plus a small profit. The bigger profits will come as your business succeeds.

8. Know the competition.

In setting a fair price for you products or services, you should look at how much other businesses who produce same or similar goods are selling their products or services for. You should also look at your competition to see if there is something you can add to your product that would make it different from your competition. Watching the competition is something you should do for the life of your business.

9. Be flexible with changes.

Life has a way of throwing changes at everyone, even those who own home-based businesses. Be willing to adjust your business to these changes. This may mean making your product with substitute ingredients, subsidizing your business with a part-time job away from home, or looking at a new market. Be one of those people who can turn life's lemons into lemonade.

10. Keep smiling.

It sounds simple, but this is very effective. Every time you talk about your product or service, make sure you are smiling and are enthusiastic. Do not cry about lazy suppliers, backed-up orders, high expenses, or the myriad of other business woes to customers or potential customers. You want your customers to associate your product or services with something happy, not gloomy.

SECTION I:

Evaluate Your Home for Business

Chapter 1

Why Start a Home-Based Business?

Although there are many reasons people start their own businesses, your reason for choosing a home-based business will be based on your own particular needs, wants, and family situation.

- ▶ **The Desire for Financial Independence**
- ▶ **The Dream of Working for Yourself**
- ▶ **The Need to be Creative**
- ▶ **Your Personal Reasons for Starting a Home-Based Business**
- ▶ **Don't Quit Your Day Job**

The Desire for Financial Independence

If your goal is to support yourself and perhaps your family, you are not alone. This reason is at the top of the list for many business owners. However, you need to know how much that support will cost.

If you do not yet have a personal or family budget, before you begin your start-up activities, you need to develop one. You must know how much money you need each month for such things as:

- rent or mortgage payments;
- general housing expenses;
- food;
- clothing;
- toiletries;
- insurance;
- car payments;
- gas and car maintenance;
- recreation;
- student and other loans;
- charitable giving;
- church, mosque, or synagogue obligations; and,
- all other living expenses.

Once you understand what your personal bottom line is, you will understand what amount of money you will need to earn from your home-based business.

You may also want to consult with a financial planner to get a good idea of what you need to earn to achieve the lifestyle you want. That will give you solid figures to use in your business plan for projected income.

Financial Freedom = Budgeting: Even businesses that eventually produce regular revenue can start out with an irregular cash flow. Making a budget will help prepare for fluctuations in your income as you start your business.

You Need to Take Care of Family Health Matters

If you or a family member has health matters that need your attention, you may want to choose a home-based business that gives you the flexibility to attend to these matters without diminishing the income you need. Learn as much as you can about future health-care costs, so you can factor those costs into the amount of income your business will need to earn to cover them.

QUICK Tip

Calculate Future Health Costs: Your doctor's office should be able to put you in touch with resources such as the *American Heart Association*, the *American Cancer Association*, or other relevant groups that can discuss possible future costs from any current illness.

The Dream of Working for Yourself

There is nothing like starting and running a business to give you a sense that you are in charge of your life. Those who have worked for someone else in a trade, profession, or other occupation can use that business experience to help in setting up their own home-based business. Those who have never worked for someone else may want to check out business start-up and management books at their local library or even take a course at a local college or technical school.

There are many other places you may want to contact to get information on starting your own home-based business.

- *Local Business Owners.* Your local chapter of the Chamber of Commerce, the *National Association of Women Business Owners*, and groups of small business owners are businesspeople who get together in order to assist each other with business advice.
- *Service Corps of Retired Executives* (S.C.O.R.E.). These retired executives can share their time and expertise with you. You can call them at 800-634-0245 to ask for the office nearest you or contact them on the Internet at **www.score.org**.

- *U.S. Small Business Administration* (SBA). Visit their website at **www.sba.gov** to find a branch near you. You may also be able to get funding for your home-based business from this organization. It is worth the time to visit this website.

You Like the Idea of Working from Home

Many people start a home-based business as a way to take charge of their lives while still fulfilling the needs of their growing family. The exchange of a long commute for a short walk down to a basement office allows you to set a schedule in which you can put aside time during the day for family obligations and crises. No longer will you need to beg your boss for those precious hours off to get your child to the pediatrician, to see your daughter star in a school play, to watch your son make the winning soccer goal, or to be a homeroom parent.

If this sounds familiar, you will need to take special care in setting up schedules and boundaries for your home-based business. You must also be sure to set aside space in your home that is just for your business. This can be your little island of quiet used just for work.

The Need to be Creative

Many people are eager to seek an environment that will free them to use their talents as they see fit. For example, if you are an artist, you may be frustrated, bored, or unhappy at your job. You may see salvation in the opportunity to set up your own business. Creative persons are often self-starters, ready to be their own boss, and eager for an outlet for their skills or training that does not have the constraints the corporate jungle imposes.

For the artist, the concern is to be able to be creative in making a product, but still perform the mundane activities needed to run a business. In the following chapters we will discuss the bare-bones activities required to run a home business. You may want to review those activities to see if you can do them in addition to producing your art.

You may not have good grounding in managing the type of business that you want to own. Read the rest of this book and try to follow our suggestions. If you are still uncomfortable with the business part of running a home-based business, consider the following three steps.

1. Take classes from the local community college or through a networking group. Classes are usually available in management, marketing, and finance. You may also be able to find a short class that is directed just at those wishing to start a home-based business.

2. Find a partner, employees, or professionals (accountants) to handle some of the business details while you supervise them.

3. Contact S.C.O.R.E. These retired executives can steer you in the direction of the type of help you need to get your business going so you can find true freedom—and make money.

Your Personal Reasons for Starting a Home-Based Business

To help define the picture of you as a business owner, ask yourself what you want to accomplish by going into business for yourself. A good place to start is by reviewing the list of questions in Figure 1.1 on the following page.

**Figure 1.1: WHY DO I WANT TO START
A HOME-BASED BUSINESS?**

- Do you have a dream to own and operate your own business?

- Did you promise yourself that one day you would start your own business?

- Do you need to work from home?

- Have you been downsized, fired, or had your position eliminated?

- Do you dislike being on unemployment benefits?

- Have you just graduated from a professional or technical school?

- Have you had several job offers, but none of them seem very interesting?

- Are you tired of the rat race that somebody else controls?

- Do you love your job, but not some major component of it (compensation, commute, etc.)?

- Are you retired and not sure what to do now?

- Will you have enough money for retirement?

- Are you a hard worker who wants to have long hours pay off for yourself, not somebody else?

- Are you bored or unhappy at work?

- Is your goal to have a lifestyle that allows you to take care of your family responsibilities—and still be productive in the workplace?

After reviewing the questions in Figure 1.1, identify your own reasons for wanting to open a home-based business. Use the following worksheet to list the reasons why you want to run your own business. List every reason that you come up with. From the most mundane (to make money), to the esoteric (to help mankind), to the frivolous (I want to impress my friends with a neat business card), write each reason down. Use the worksheet supplied in Figure 1.2 to organize your thoughts.

Figure 1.2: WHY DO I WANT TO OPERATE MY OWN HOME-BASED BUSINESS?

RANK	REASON

Once you are sure that you have listed every reason, rank the reasons in the column provided. Pay particular attention to your top ten reasons. These are your basic motivators.

You now have a list of goals for your home-based business.

Don't Quit Your Day Job

Having a day job may be a realistic choice during the start-up phase of your home-based business. This is especially true if the income from your new business is below what you need to cover your personal and business expenses. You may also be able to meet your personal and business expenses if you have an outside source of income such as a retirement check, a family member's income, savings, or inheritance. (To make ends meet, a computer programmer in our neighborhood works evenings and weekends for a local tech company while he and a friend put together a ".com" enterprise.)

Chapter

Kinds of Home-Based Businesses

Many businesses can be done out of your home—from supplying a service to others, to running a craft business, to working in a home-based franchise.

- ▶ **Providing Services to Others**
- ▶ **Professional Businesses**
- ▶ **Craft Businesses**
- ▶ **Child-Oriented Businesses**
- ▶ **Foods and Edibles**
- ▶ **eBay**
- ▶ **Portable Businesses**
- ▶ **Franchises**
- ▶ **Getting Ideas for a Home Business**

Providing Services to Others

The service industry continues to grow despite economic downturns and higher unemployment. A business that provides a service has a statistically greater likelihood of success than a business that produces a product. Many owners of home-based, small businesses are taking advantage of the need for services by providing a service that others either do not want to bother with or that is very time consuming.

Services for Other Businesses

Businesses contract with other businesses for services all the time. The accounting department calls an office supply store to order more accounting pads. The computer department calls a local software store to order the latest release of software.

There is an unending list of services that a small home business can provide to other businesses. Some services include: office cleaning, event planning, catering, coffee service or vending, and pick up and delivery.

Consultants. One of the first things to come to mind in this category is the consultant that a business hires, usually in the computer-related area. It is not unusual for a computer expert, who was downsized due to the economy, to return to his or her original job as a consultant. The benefit for the business of hiring the consultant is that it does not have to pay employee benefits. The benefit for the consultant is that he or she has control over when and where he or she works.

QUICK Tip

A Special Note for Consultants: If your goal is to use your expertise in a consulting business, think through (with great specificity) how you will define your consulting services. Because the role of consultant varies from industry to industry and your expertise might very well apply to many types of industries, it is critical to know what your marketplace expectations are. You will need to craft your practice based on the vision for your business, as well as the expectations of potential clients.

Contract Opportunities. Law firms may contract with a business to file documents in certain courts. Doctor's offices may contract with a business to hand deliver medical essentials or files between a hospital and the doctor's office. Many of the services that businesses pay for are done on their premises or involve traveling to their premises. These services can include painting, decorating, taking care of plants, warehousing, and shipping.

Specialty Jobs. There are certain jobs you may be able to do from home as a business. You may be able to perform computer research from your home computer. Some businesses, especially in the publishing area, allow people to work from home writing manuscripts or reading and reviewing others' manuscripts. The type of service you can perform for another business is only limited by your imagination and its ability to pay.

Services Done for Individuals

Most people have something they hate to do and many times they are willing pay someone else to do it. Things like walking the dog, cleaning up after the dog, taking the dog to the vet, and taking care of the dog when the owners are out of town are just a handful of things that would appeal to one segment of the population—dog owners. Dog and cat owners are also potential customers for a house-sitter—someone who stays in the house and cares for the animals while the owner is out of town.

You may be able to market yourself as someone who stays inside a home to let in the carpenters, utility installers, or TV cable installers. Many people will gladly pay someone so that they do not lose a day's work for the "sometime between 9 and 5" appointments that many installers require.

Outside the Home. Families with two working parents may be happy to pay for someone to mow the lawn or do other outside chores so the family can spend some quality weekend time together. Many homeowners would not even consider going up a ladder to clean leaves from gutters, paint trim, paint the house, or hang holiday lights. The same thing goes for the interior of the house. Any work around the house can become a potential service business.

Inside the Home. Other potential service businesses are inside a home. Many people will pay a person who can refinish furniture, especially old furniture with a sentimental value. The thousands who have purchased homes that require rehabbing are also potential customers for someone who refinishes old woodwork or floors; strips off old wallpaper; repairs plaster walls; or, does general carpentry.

Minor Personal Assistance. Many people are now caring for elderly and infirmed family members. Most would gladly pay for someone to come in and care for the family member, even if it is just for an hour. People who have problems getting around due to an injury or disease may need someone to come in to prepare a meal. As our society ages, there will be more people who need minor assistance. This is a time when an individual service business can flourish.

One last thought on individual service businesses. Recently, stories were in the news about a service for breaking up with your boyfriend or girlfriend. Did you know there is even a business that will wait in line for you at concerts and movie theaters that have open seating? There are people who will pay someone else to handle almost any annoying or time-consuming project.

Advantages of a Service Business

The biggest plus for starting a service business is that everyone, even businesses, needs services. There will always be a certain market for a given service. As the culture and economy change, so do the numbers of services that we ask others to perform. Many aging baby boomers have plenty of disposable income and are willing to pay someone else to handle specific aspects of their lives.

In addition, many service businesses can be started on a shoestring. Supplies can be bought cheaply at the big warehouse stores or over the Internet, without having to order the enormous quantities that are usually associated with buying wholesale.

CASE STUDY: **Growing a Service Business**

Amy needed a second job. During the day she was a receptionist for a local dentist, but the job didn't pay much. Amy decided to start an office cleaning business for small offices at night. She contacted several small businesses in her area and she got three contracts. Amy bought a few cleaning supplies at her local grocery store and supplemented that with her own homemade vinegar mix for cleaning glass. She brought rags from home and used the plastic bags from her groceries for garbage pick up.

Disadvantages of a Service Business

One serious challenge is getting your service known. Another concern may be building the trust of your clients, especially if your business involves being in your client's home alone. You may need to have yourself and your employees *bonded*. (Being bonded is handled through an insurance company that specializes in researching a person's background and guaranteeing that person's honesty—to a point.)

Marketing

If you are providing services for businesses, use mailings with brochures and your business card. About once a month, contact the business by phone or mail. Know the names of who in the business can help you. For individual services, keep your advertising simple. Most new business owners prefer to use an ad in the local paper that is run every week.

Professional Businesses

The sad truth about our economy is that everyone in every type job can be terminated, laid-off, or forced to quit. This includes what most people refer to as professionals—those who are required to have an advanced degree to do their work. It is also true that professionals, like the rest of us, get to that point in life when they want to cut back. Everyone, no matter how great the degree, can suffer from burnout, become tired of working for someone else, or just want to slow down. If you are a professional, you too can work from home. In many professions it is even common to begin the road to a large business by working out of your home.

Legal

For years, attorneys have worked out of their home. The extra room, the den, and the garage turned into an office have all become places to practice law. The home-based attorney sometimes provides yet another service to his or her clients—house calls. For the disabled and elderly, an attorney who will come to them is a godsend.

Many solo practitioners begin working at home. It is the place to build a practice without the initial expenses for an office, furniture, supplies, staff, etc. With a computer and an answering machine, a solo attorney can handle cases in the same professional manner as the attorney who is paying thousands of dollars a month for a fancy office. It is the attorney's abilities with the clients and in the courts that matter—not his or her office.

Besides attorneys, paralegals and other legal assistants can work from their home. Even the smallest law firms may hire someone to make an occasional court appearance or to file documents in different courts. Those who specialize in performing legal research may be able to do the computer research and write research reports from home. Also, many of the stenographers that are used by lawyers to capture statements in hearings and depositions are able to transcribe their notes at home.

Medical

Doctors have a long history of working from their homes. The image of the country doctor with an office in his or her home is becoming more of a reality, especially for those doctors who have moved into smaller towns.

In addition to doctors, other medical professionals can work from their homes. Nurses with the proper licensing can contract with patients and patients' families for individual care. In this case, the nurse goes to the elderly or disabled patient who is bedridden. (As the number of elderly people increase, the need for medical professionals who make house calls will also increase.)

Accounting, Bookkeeping, and Other Business Jobs

Many accountants start out working on tax returns from their home. One accountant we know became so successful that he bought the house next door to live in, rehabbed the original home into all offices, and hired several accountants to work for him.

Another area of financial work that can be done from home is bookkeeping. Bookkeepers are those who enter the financial data from a business onto a computer spreadsheet or onto paper. They also analyze the financial data and prepare the financial statements for the company. Most of this function can be done from the bookkeeper's home. Some companies that use non-employee bookkeepers require that they enter the financial data at the company's location. Once the data is entered, computer reports are generated and the bookkeeper can use these to prepare the statements from home.

Many former corporate secretaries and typists work from their home typing documents, especially for students. While most students have their own computer, some just do not have the speed required to quickly produce a multipage term paper or thesis. Another area for a small home business can be producing professional presentations and brochures.

Freelancing

Working as a freelancer (consultant) is becoming very desirable for both the business doing the hiring *and* the worker. A freelancer is usually defined as a person who does the work of an employee for a contracted period of time, for a set cost, but who does not receive benefits such as vacation, insurance, 401(k), etc. In legal terms, you are an *independent contractor*.

The businesses using this type of worker can save money. The business gets a worker without having to pay the benefits an employee requires. If the amount of work needed to be done drops, an independent contractor may be able to be let go without the concern of a wrongful termination lawsuit. Also, many independent contractors pay their own taxes and withholdings. That way, the business saves money on tax processing.

Monetary Benefits: For the freelancer, independent contractor, or consultant, the major benefits are a higher salary and the freedom to set his or her own hours. This type of work can provide experience in a new profession without making an employee commitment.

How do you fit being a freelancer into a home business? Easy. Your home becomes your primary office, with your product being you. You market your skills along with the benefits that the employer will receive from using a nonemployee. Figure 2.1 describes the items you will need to maintain a freelance business from your home.

Figure 2.1: BASIC ITEMS YOU WILL NEED TO DO FREELANCING FROM YOUR HOME

- Health insurance for yourself and family
- Contracts for deals between you and other businesses
- A brochure describing your abilities (you can do this on your own computer)
- A good calendar to keep track of your appointments

Many businesspeople are considered freelancers, independent contractors, or consultants. Many professions have been using this type of worker for a long time, especially in construction, carpentry, residential painting, computer programming, computer analysts, accounting, bookkeeping, data entry, and deliveries. In the last five years, many additional professions have also begun to benefit from this type of worker.

Advantages for the Home Professional

There are advantages for the professional who is considering starting a home business. It is a way to work in the profession without being tied to a boss or corporation. For some people it is an inexpensive way to begin a career; for others it can be beginning steps into retirement. The sense of being successful on your own independent terms is extremely positive.

Disadvantages for the Home Professional

A professional has certain legal requirements that must be met, no matter how large or small the business. For example, many professionals are required to take classes annually to keep their skills current. For a person who is working from his or her home without a partner or other employees, this means that the office is closed for the duration of this education. In addition, while this continuing education may be only a small percentage of the expenses of a large corporation, an individual working from his or her home may find that continuing education can wipe out a large portion of the profit.

Another disadvantage may be inadvertently putting your home and family in danger, if you have clients coming to your home office. However, a home-based business owner can keep both home and family safe while successfully managing a business by taking active steps to keep the business separate from your home and family. The level of separation depends on your business and your potential clients. Figure 2.2 addresses security issues that you should consider when starting your business.

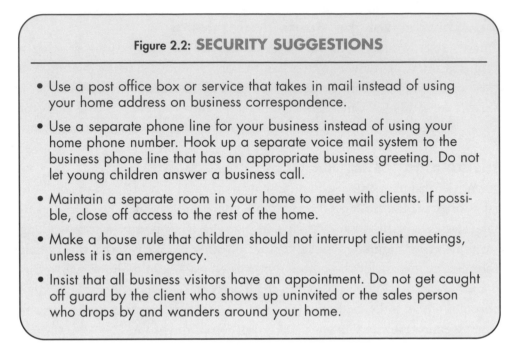

Figure 2.2: SECURITY SUGGESTIONS

- Use a post office box or service that takes in mail instead of using your home address on business correspondence.

- Use a separate phone line for your business instead of using your home phone number. Hook up a separate voice mail system to the business phone line that has an appropriate business greeting. Do not let young children answer a business call.

- Maintain a separate room in your home to meet with clients. If possible, close off access to the rest of the home.

- Make a house rule that children should not interrupt client meetings, unless it is an emergency.

- Insist that all business visitors have an appointment. Do not get caught off guard by the client who shows up uninvited or the sales person who drops by and wanders around your home.

Craft Businesses

Are you a crafter—someone who scours the craft stores scooping up yarn, needlepoint, felt, sequins, and those little wooden sticks? Do you give home-made gifts to family and friends? Is your favorite time when you can sit and stitch on your latest counted cross-stitch kit? If that describes you, you may be able to turn your hobby into an actual business that makes money.

Assessing Your Craft Abilities

Many people enjoy doing handmade crafts. If you are one of those people, you may be able to make a living crafting. You know what craft you love to do. It is probably the one you spend most of your time on, are most proud of, and have given friends and family at least one of. Unlike people who are not sure what they can do, you know what you want to do—you just need to find a way to make a living at it.

Look closely at what craft you really enjoy doing and what craft you do well. You may have many craft specialties, such as scrapbooking, knitting, crocheting, needle pointing, or counted cross-stitch; however, which of your craft products make others say "Wow"? Do you make your own patterns? Is there something about your favorite craft that makes yours unique? (Quality products that are unique will sell.)

Along with creating a product that pleases others enough to spend their money on it, which of your craft products can you make multiples of in a short period of time? For example, the quilt that took you five years to finish is beautiful, but can you produce enough high quality quilts in a short period of time to make money?

Pricing

What about the price? Consider that the quilt took you 1,300 hours to complete (which is one hour a day five days a week for those five years). In order to get $1 an hour for your time, you would need to charge $1,300 to buy the quilt. If you charge $650, you are valuing your time at 50¢ an hour, at $325 your time is now worth 25¢ an hour. At $325 for a handmade quilt, you are now competing with major stores that sell handmade quilts for under $250 and machine made quilts for as low as $50.

There is a great deal of difference between enjoying a craft such as knitting and being able to make a living selling your knitted creations. Crafting is an industry that is one of the toughest to make a decent living in. Why? Many people do not value a homemade craft. They see the number of do-it-yourself craft kits, go into craft stores, and assume that they can do just as good a job as a professional crafter. This perception of not valuing a homemade craft translates for the crafter as not being able to charge appropriately for the time and care taken with the project.

QUICK Tip

Setting a Price: Before you set up that knitting machine or open a scrapbook shop, look at how others are pricing their crafts. Go to craft fairs to get an idea on how similar products are being priced. Look at prices for similar products on the Internet, especially on eBay where individuals can sell their products directly. Finally, look at commercial manufacturing to see if there is a similar product already in the market place.

Remember, it is not only the cost of your time that you must figure into a price, but also the cost of materials. When setting the price of your craft, start with the cost of materials (including shipping of the materials to you) and then add the cost of your time.

CASE STUDY: The Cost of Raw Materials

Mary, an avid knitter, had to raise the price of her best-selling product as the price of imported angora yarn skyrocketed. Soon her local suppliers stopped carrying such expensive yarn and she was forced to buy the yarn out of state, which added more to the price. Eventually, the cost to make a knitted product out of this expensive yarn became more than the customer would pay.

Your Market

Your market boils down to who will buy your goods. Handmade items have their own market. If you are planning to make this your home business, you need to do research to see where that market is.

Your primary interest is selling at craft fairs and shows. You know that the customers coming to a craft fair are already interested in handmade items. Many cities hold craft fairs in conjunction with local events. Some craft fairs are done by invitation only. In this case, you submit a sample of what you make and it is judged on specific criteria. Invitation-only craft fairs usually look for a variety of different types of handmade items, especially if the selling space is limited. A craft fair that can only hold fifty crafters is probably not going to invite ten crafters who knit baby blankets.

Sometimes a church, civic group, or charity will hold a craft fair. A percentage (or all) of the money you make at this event may go to the organizers. However, supporting this event may make your name and product visible to more people.

Along with craft fairs and shows, some cities have tourist areas where handcrafted goods and tasks from the past are showcased 365 days of the year. Many of these areas have a *consignment store* for local crafters. This is a store where you can sell you crafts to the public. The store provides the space for your goods and takes a portion of the proceeds. This type of store is a great way to determine if there is a market for your goods without a significant investment. Again, the customers who frequent the consignment stores in the tourist areas are already convinced about the value of handcrafted goods and they want a special remembrance of their trip.

CASE STUDY: Consignment Stores

In Morro Bay, California, there is a store in the tourist section by the bay. It has a great variety of handcrafted items—all made by local Morro Bay residents. The store takes a percentage of what is paid and the rest is given to the crafters.

Another group of potential customers are those who do not necessarily care about the skill it takes to make handcrafted items, but are looking for good quality, unique products. You may be able to sell your unique items to these people through small boutiques, hotel gift shops, or a shop that specializes in unique products.

CASE STUDY: Making Unique Products with Added Value

One Christmas, a young mother designed and knitted hats for herself and the other women in her family. She became so good at knitting that she could produce one hat in a couple of days. She decided to sell her hats in a winter resort's gift shop on consignment. She was able to sell even more hats when she added mittens to match.

One way to sell to those customers who do not normally look for handmade items is to personalize the product. An embroidered sampler with the date of the wedding and the names of the bride and groom makes a great wedding gift. A baby blanket with the newborn's name and birth date sewn in would tug at any new grandparent's heart. A Christmas ornament for our first Christmas, baby's first Christmas, or just the names of the family put on it could also make a profitable product.

Find New Markets: Once you identify your main market, you may also decide to sell your hand-made goods on the Internet or through eBay.

Teaching a Craft

Many people envy those who have mastered a craft. Old crafts have become associated with the good old days and many people long to learn how to do them. Skills and techniques for doing certain things that are now considered crafty are often no longer passed down from mother to daughter or father to son as they once were. It is no wonder then, that the number of classes that teach specific crafts have increased. In many areas, junior colleges, park districts, senior centers, even adult education facilities have added classes in knitting, candlemaking, woodworking, and ceramics.

You may also be able to teach your craft at an event such as a county fair or church bazaar. There are also large stores that sell craft materials. Many of these stores provide classes showing customers how to use their materials.

If you are interested in teaching your craft, contact the locations in your area that are currently providing craft classes. You may also want to consider holding classes in your home. Home classes are usually limited to a handful of people so the teacher can really help each student. (Some home classes include tools (needles, hooks, etc.), patterns, or materials. Other home classes ask the student to select and bring their own materials.)

Advantages to a Craft Business

The biggest positive for owning a craft business is the pleasure of doing what you love and seeing other people love something you have actually created. There is great satisfaction in having a stranger praise what you have made. In addition, it is also an easy business to get into while you are working a full-time job.

Disadvantages to a Craft Business

There are many negatives about running a homecraft business. You may find yourself always making inventory. While this means that everything you make is selling, it may take so long to build up stock that you are unable to sell at fairs and bazaars.

On the flip side, you may love what you create, but it just doesn't sell well. Many customers look at handcrafts with an extremely critical eye because they feel that they could do it themselves. Finally, you may learn to hate the craft. Be honest, if you are required to turn out fourteen potholders a day, how long will it be before you feel this is a chore?

Child-Oriented Businesses

There are options for those who want to center their work around children. However, along with options come a myriad of regulations and laws that go along with this type of business. (This is not an area for the unprepared.)

This section is a mere overview of a child-oriented business and the issues that go along with such a business. You will need to do lots of research if you are seriously considering selling anything for children or providing services for children.

Day Care

Day care used to be so simple. It was even called by a friendly name—baby-sitting. Now this area of child care is scrutinized and in most states regulated by law. This is one type of home business that looks deceptively easy, but can turn into an emotional and financial nightmare.

In every neighborhood there are mothers of children who stay at home to care for their own children and think they could easily take care of a few more. While physically this may be true, if you are seriously considering caring for children in you home, do some research.

First, look at your state, county, and town's laws about day care. Many more states are requiring that day care operators be licensed. Along with that license are additional safety rules, insurance requirements, and, possible inspections.

Second, ask questions about your liability. An attorney or your insurance agent should be able to help you with this. Find out if you are liable under your state's law when—one child injures another; one child passes on a serious illness to another; a child sustains a minor injury at your facility; parents bring you into the middle of their divorce; or, any of the other issues that a day care operator faces every day. Look at areas in which the law says you are liable and then see if you can obtain insurance to cover that liability.

Alert!

Insurance: Your current home insurance policy will likely not be extensive enough to protect you if you decide to take care of children in your home. Be sure to check with your insurance agent before you open your home for business.

Third, assess the portion of your house you intend to use for the day care. While it may be childproof sufficiently for your children, the rambunctious 3-year-old down the block may easily cause damage to your home and him- or herself. Make sure that you and your family can live with the changes that must be made.

Alert!

You Are Not My Mommy: Think twice, three times, a hundred times, until you and your family are sure, without reservations, that you want to run a day care facility. While those little naughty acts of children may bring a smile to your face, how will you feel about a room full of screaming little strangers that defy you because "You are not my Mommy!"

Do not forget to get input from your older children and other family members who are living at home. The rule of thumb is everyone agrees to this or do not do it. This is for your protection. Unfortunately, there have been several cases in which charges of child abuse were brought against a day care operator due to the actions of an older child or an adult who was still living in the home. Most of these types of charges are later proven to be untrue. However, this type of scandal can destroy a family and all their financial security. Even a minor charge of negligence or abuse that is later determined to be false can cost a day care operator thousands of dollars in attorney's fees and lost business.

Teaching or Tutoring

If day care is not an option, there are many other home businesses you can operate that will allow you to work with children. Teaching and tutoring are very important. Some teachers spend their entire summer in one-on-one tutoring for a few students to prepare them for the next year. Children who have missed a significant portion of school due to illness during the school year may be able to make that time up and stay in the same grade by utilizing this type of one-on-one tutoring.

There are also teachers who tutor students during the school year to help the students understand a particular subject and bring up their grades. Of course, there is also the kindly piano teacher who teaches a select group of budding piano virtuosos from his or her home. If you can teach, this may be a very good home business to get into. The start-up costs are very low and the rewards are great.

Products for Children

A home business can produce many items for children, such as toys, child-furniture, clothing, holders to display children's awards, scrapbooks, etc.

> **QUICK Tip**
>
> Parents Demand Quality in Materials: Parents insist on the very best for their children, therefore your product must be of the highest quality. For example, if you are making wooden toys for children, secure all pieces so that nothing can fall off. Keep all pieces larger than what would fit down a child's throat.

An interesting area of items to make for children is clothing. Parents may be more than willing to pay for handmade special clothing such as christening outfits, first communion outfits, bas and bar mitzvah outfits, or other clothes for special events. (Special event clothing can extend from birth until the child marries.)

CASE STUDY: Make Special Occasion Clothes

One seamstress we know makes extra money by creating unique wedding veils that contain veiling and antique lace from both the bride's mother and grandmother's wedding veils.

Advantages and Disadvantages

The need for businesses that produce items for and provide services for children is increasing on a daily basis. We are in the middle of a baby boom and today's parents are happy to spend money on their children.

That is both a positive and a negative. It is positive because the potential market is increasing, but it is also negative because everyone, even the large corporations, knows these facts. This means that your competition will be everyone from the home business next door to that gigantic international corporation.

Alert!

You May Need a License: Depending upon your state and local laws, your child-oriented home business may require additional licenses, fees, and inspection costs. All of these can be negatives to a home business' bottom line.

Foods and Edibles

You have the best recipe for butterscotch cookies known to man. It has been handed down in your family for the last hundred years. At every event you are invited to, people ask you to bring your homemade cookies. Now you want to retire from the corporate life and begin selling these cookies. Before you turn in your two-weeks notice to your boss, here are some things to consider about the market you are about to enter.

QUICK Tip

A Special Note for Inventors: Inventors need to know that the process to get a patent can take more than a few months. It may be easier, financially, if you have a source of income while you wait. This will put you in a position to develop your plans; assess your market; identify the people you will need; and, pay your rent.

Your Market

In the majority of major grocery stores, shelf space is sold to the makers of the food product. That's right. Major food manufacturers must pay the grocery store for shelf space. Do not expect your local grocery store to put your butterscotch cookies in a prominent shelf space, no matter how great they taste. This is especially true if your product is competing with other major manufactures that can produce similar goods at half the cost.

In business terms, the relationship between the major grocery store and the major goods manufacturer *limits* your market. This requires additional work on your part to find a *nontraditional market* for your butterscotch cookies. You may be able to sell them from small food stores, delis, stores that only carry snack foods such as resort gift stores, or health food stores (if your ingredients apply). One problem is that many of the smaller food stores, like those in tourist areas or along interstate highways, are now attempting to cash in on the same concept of selling shelf space as the major grocery stores. It may take a considerable amount of effort to find a store where you do not have to buy a place on a shelf.

Give Free Samples to the Storeowner:
One way to get on the good side of the storeowner is to give them (for free) a quantity of your product to be used as samples for the public. Make sure that you provide enough of the product so that the owner and his or her employees get more than a taste with sufficient quantity left to put out for the public.

Many home business gourmet food makers begin by selecting a few stores, placing both a tray of samples and packaged products ready for purchase in each store, then, every day going to each store to refill the sample trays and restock the inventory.

Alert!

Be Aware of Your Ingredients: Make sure that your product can sit out on a sample tray without spoilage.

Getting a product in the store is only the first step. You also must service that store on a regular basis. For food products this may mean that you visit each store several times a week or even daily. Your competition, the big food manufacturers, employ a work force to do this same function. Once you can determine how your product sells in a store, you can then set a regular schedule. Servicing stores also entails making good on items returned to the store and being ready to restock the inventory without delay.

Storeowners Can Control Your Profits: Remember that the storeowner can control your profits by limiting the exposure of your product to the public. Excellent customer service is the key to building a positive relationship with the storeowner.

Other nontraditional places to sell your edibles are on the Internet, at local fairs, at church bazaars, or at any store that will put up a small display at the cash register.

CASE STUDY: Placing Your Product in Different Locations

One superstar began by selling small bags of homemade candy from the gas station her parents owned. She went on to a newspaper shop in a major office building and then to making up special candy boxes for businesses in that office building to send to their customers. Her business is now concentrated on producing corporate gifts for businesses to send to their customers in celebration of holidays, birthdays, and other important events.

What's It Made From

Another major issue with making any kind of edible is the ingredients used. We are becoming very health conscious. People who used to eat anything are now reading the labels and looking for information. It is the norm for even homemade edibles to contain a list of ingredients. This is done because in many areas of the country this is the law. Local laws and

FDA directives must be followed, especially when you are producing something people are going to ingest.

You know your ingredients. Make a list of what is in the item, print that list on a sticky label, and put the label on the package of your product. If the package is too small to hold a label, use a small font when printing, re-package using a larger quantity of goods, tie an ingredients list tag to the package, or include an ingredient list with each sale. While you are not required to give the quantity of the ingredients, you should list the ingredients in order of quantity (for example, is it cheese and macaroni or macaroni and cheese). The government site **www.fda.gov** may be of some help in this.

Alert!

List Your Ingredients: People who are highly allergic to peanuts can get very ill or even die from ingesting even one morsel of peanut or peanut oil. Other people have medical reactions to flour, dairy, chocolate, etc. In addition to addressing your customer's needs, you must also protect your company from liability and bad press.

Sanitation

Making something for another person to eat is a great joy and responsibility. The joy is something that every cook feels when someone enjoys food they have prepared. The responsibility has become more intense and, in this litigious society, is even more important to the life of your company. Every aspect of sanitation must be followed when preparing food for your customers. There are books, free pamphlets from the government, and courses that teach sanitation in food preparation.

Think about your feelings when one of your children eats food made by someone other than you. You want each ingredient to be touched only by washed hands, properly cleaned, free of contaminants or foreign objects, cooked thoroughly, and not sold when it is past its expiration date. These are the golden standards for making edibles for the public.

Packaging

Packaging of a product can result in an impulse buy or can cause the customer to bypass the product. Have you ever seen those individual cookies for sale by the cash register of your local convenience store? Which is more appealing—the one with a tight clear plastic cover that is sealed with an ingredients sticker, or the one in a tiny loose baggy that allows the crumbs to adhere to the bag so that you really cannot see the cookie? Think about the presentation of your product when you are not there and how your package will protect the product. Packages should show the product at its best, while still protecting it from being crushed, bruised, or bug-infested.

 **Tell the Customer Who You Are:** In addition to putting the ingredient list on the package, include a label that contains the name of your company, plus a contact phone number or email address so the customer can order more.

eBay

For those who don't know, *eBay* is an online place for a person or business to market goods in an auction style. There are thousands of categories of products on eBay and it is very popular. For those looking for rare or unusual items or for what was formerly referred to as surplus or out of season items, eBay is great. It is so popular that another class of businesses has been created to deal with the auction site. These businesses range from places that will help the bidders become the high bidder and buyer, to a business that will list, sell, and ship your product.

Because of the success that many people have had unloading their wares via eBay, businesses are now using this service. Initially, it was the home businesses and small businesses. Now, however, there is a significant increase in major corporations using eBay to test new products, unload excess products, and to introduce another market to their goods. This is where some of the problems have developed.

For a long time many success stories of home business selling on eBay were heard. Home businesses did so much business that soon they were looking for a nonhome location and hiring employees. However, recently there have been some very disturbing rumblings from many of the small business that are already using eBay.

As more big businesses have signed on, eBay has changed. Fees to sell have increased and policies and services have changed. Other complaints include the large number of big businesses who are competing with the home businesses. Big businesses can offer products at a greater discount than can most small businesses.

The bottom line for using eBay to sell your products is research. It is still a good way to see if a brand new product will have any buyers. It still appeals to many people who regularly buy things from the Internet. Selling anything on eBay is and never has been a piece of cake. Just the data entry can be a pain. Now there is the additional pain of higher fees when you do sell. If you feel comfortable selling your product via eBay, great, then do it. However, remember not everyone uses eBay, and your potential customers may be one of those groups that just do not look at eBay at all.

Portable Businesses

One of the hottest, new type of business is the *portable business*. This type of business opportunity allows retirees, military and corporate spouses, and those married to Foreign Service Officers, who live from one move to the next, to take charge of their lives and still meet their family obligations. Portable businesses can earn money no matter how often the owner moves and no matter where he or she moves.

Alert!

Know the Local Laws: If you make your home business a portable one, there may be local laws that control your business. Make sure you find out what they are before you set up your operation.

E-commerce and consulting are two great potential portable businesses. Small businesses need to outsource things such as consumer brochures and pamphlets, reports, and online instruction manuals. Portable opportunities are out there and are limited only by your skills, interests, and imagination. Your portability possibilities are enhanced by the following:

- cellular and satellite technologies;
- laptop computers and portable printers;
- email and websites;
- banking features, such as worldwide wiring of cash, automatic payment of your bills, and direct deposit of some checks;
- the availability of overnight letter and package delivery in most parts of the world; and,
- mailbox services that will forward or send your mail to you just about anywhere on earth.

Take advantage of all these opportunities, if possible. If not, focus on the ones that best suit your immediate needs.

Franchises

Franchises are a way to buy into a business that is already established. The business may provide certain incentives for a person to buy a franchise such as: advertising, marketing, a listing on the corporate website, office supplies, equipment, customer referrals, and association with a business that the public knows.

To help you decide if a franchise is right for you, plan to do extensive research. First, you will need to locate all the franchises that are available for home-based businesses and pick out those that match your needs. A great place to start is with the *Entrepreneur Magazine*, **www.entrepreneur.com**. In the March 2005 issue, this magazine listed information on the top 105 home-based franchises. This list can be found at **www.entrepreneur.com/franzone/ listings/home101/0,5833,,00.html**.

The second step is to research the particular franchise that you are interested in. Most of the home-based franchises have websites and toll-free numbers to obtain additional information. The third step is to get an attorney to review the franchise agreement prior to you signing it. Each franchise agreement is different and may contain hidden costs. Before you spend the money to buy a franchise and sign an agreement that may cost you additional funds, it is important that you know what you are signing.

Getting Ideas for a Home Business

Other places you can go to get ideas about what you might be good at doing include the following.

- Wander into a variety of businesses and talk with the owner. Ask if he or she were starting a business today, which one would he or she choose and why.
- Check out the library or bookstores for books about people who have started businesses.
- Take classes. For example, community colleges and community centers often have classes from aerobics (learn to be an instructor) to woodworking.
- Learn a new skill.
- Identify trends that could lead to a product or service that interests you.
- Read national publications such as the *Wall Street Journal*, *New York Times*, the *Washington Post*, *U.S.A. Today*, *Business Week*, and *Time*. (Most public libraries subscribe to these publications.)
- Watch business programs on television.
- Go online and check out business' home pages.

Advantages and Disadvantages of a Home Business

Running your own business from home is usually a positive. You set your own hours, all the businesses profits go to you, and you have the pride of saying, *I own my own business*. If you do the preliminary work before opening the business and continue that work, your business will be a success. The extent of your success is determined by your ability to prepare.

As with all roses, running a home business also has thorns. Being at home makes you vulnerable to those distractions such as laundry, cleaning, cooking, your children, and the phone.

In addition, when the business is yours, you never stop thinking about it. The business will color your world for good or bad. When profits are down, you mope around the house; when customers complain, you can become a grump to your family. However, when you get that first big order, you are so happy you even kiss the dog.

Is running your own home business worth the headaches? The answer is a resounding YES!

Chapter

Is Your Home the Right Place for a Business?

While you may dream about working from home, your city or town may not agree that it is an appropriate and legal place for a business.

- ▶ **Zoning and Other Local Laws**
- ▶ **Business Address**
- ▶ **Image**
- ▶ **Home Office Furniture**
- ▶ **Home Office Equipment**
- ▶ **Phone Lines**
- ▶ **Parking**

Zoning and Other Local Laws

Before you make the decision to open a home-based business, you need to do some research of the laws in your city. Local laws may prevent you from having a commercial business in your home, especially if that means increased traffic in your area. If your home-based business includes commercial vehicles, either as part of your business or as customers, you will need to check if your city has any weight restrictions for your street.

Gated Community or Home Association Rules

Those who own or rent a co-op, condo, town house, or apartment that is located within a gated community or homeowners association may have another layer of rules to follow in addition to the local laws of the city, county, and state. You will need to determine if your landlord, home association, or management company has any rules that effect or restrict having a business in your home.

If you are renting, the first place to check is your rental agreement or lease. If there are no restrictions, your next step is to check the association or management rules that everyone who occupies a unit must abide by. After you are sure that the owner, association, or management will allow a home-based business, then research the local laws of your city.

Local Business License

Some cities require that home-based businesses register with city hall and obtain a business license. Others require that the home-based business pay a surcharge or charge certain taxes. In order to determine your particular situation, contact your city hall and ask to speak with a small business compliance officer, someone familiar with laws that effect local businesses, or the person designated to handle questions from local businesses.

QUICK Tip

Find a Local, Small Business Champion: Every city or town government has someone who is familiar with the local laws and is eager to assist local businesses. If you want to find the information on your own, check your county, city, or town website.

Business Address

Can you use your home address for your business? Yes, but you may not want to. Many home-based business owners do not want to see clients in their home. It is up to you, your family, and your type of business.

There are several options for the home-based business in avoiding use of the home address. You can set up a postal box at the post office or at package stores that offer this service. (The only down side to this is having to use the designation "P.O. Box" as the business address.) For most of the package stores, your business address will be the street address of this store *plus* the box number. Many home businesses translate this into a street address—the word *suite* and then the box number. Before you do this, check with the package store to see if this is legal in your state.

A company called *HQ Global Workplaces* is a favorite solution to the business address issue. You can contact the company at its website, **www.hqglobal.com**, or by phone at 888-271-4615. HQ Global provides a business presence in a particular location without the expense of setting up your own office. Basically it leases an area in an office building; sets up individual offices; and, then provides complete business services to its clients. Depending on the level of service you select, HQ Global can:

- provide a business telephone line;
- have your line answered by a person;
- provide voice mail;
- provide you with a street address for mail;
- forward your mail to you;
- provide you with a variety of offices and meeting rooms on a per hour or per day basis; and,
- provide administrative staff to assist you in just about every aspect of starting up and running a business.

There are many positives for this type of set up, with the main one being the safety and privacy for your family. The second is that HQ usually picks outstanding office buildings in which to lease. These are the types of office buildings that most small businesses could not afford to rent, especially when starting out. Another benefit is that if you need help for things like sending out mailings, planning a business meeting, etc., there are professionals there to assist you.

What if there is not an HQ Global Workplace near you? You may still want to consider them if only to answer your business phone, collect your mail, and then ship that mail on to your home. Otherwise you may be able to contract with a local business landlord to allow you to use his or her building as your business address.

Image

Determine whether you are in a business that needs an *image* or certain address to establish credibility. It is conceivable that image may be so important in some businesses that a home-based business is not a realistic consideration. You need to learn that as soon as possible; definitely while you are still in your planning phase. No sense wasting time, money, and dreams on a guaranteed loser.

Find out if having a presence in a certain part of town, perhaps among other similar businesses, is critical for success in your line of work. In some industries, no one pays attention to where your business is located. In other industries or professions, if you do not have an address on a particular street, you will not have the image that customers expect.

CASE STUDY: Being in the Right Location

Susan opened her art gallery in her home so she would not have to commute downtown in traffic. She took that money saved from commuting and added it to her advertising budget. She did pretty well that first year, but it became apparent during the second year that her location was hurting her. Twice a year, the downtown arts neighborhood sponsored an Art Crawl. All the galleries were open in the evening during the Art Crawl and each served refreshments; some even had entertainment. The Art Crawl had become a part of the social scene in the city and the galleries that participated were developing incredible reputations. Susan decided the money she spent on advertising would be better spent on higher rent for space in the arts neighborhood.

Figure 3.1: COMMUNICATING A PROFESSIONAL IMAGE OF YOUR BUSINESS

If you are working from home, a professional business image may be important if you regularly invite customers to your office. Some factors to consider include the following:

- a separate, dedicated phone line that is answered by you or someone else with a business-like greeting;

- voice mail or an answering service to respond to calls when you cannot;

- a name and/or logo for your business that is consistently used on business cards, letterhead, and other marketing materials;

- an address (actual or post office box) that is consistent with a business-like image;

- access to your office through surroundings that reinforce your business' image; and,

- a clean, organized, appropriately furnished space for client meetings.

Home Office Furniture

If the space in your home you will be using for office or paper work is tiny and you have a limited start-up budget, take heart. Your initial furniture needs will probably be quite small. You might be able to make do with whatever pieces are around the house. However, do not be shortsighted. Make your space comfortable enough so that you will want to go there to work and do the tasks that you must. Lighting, an ergonomically correct chair, and a desk should be your minimal concerns.

 **Need Files:** Office supply stores sell large hard plastic storage boxes for files that are sturdy, have covers to keep out dust, and are an inexpensive alternative to a file cabinet.

The home-based businessperson often has to meet the challenge of keeping business matters private and segregated from the rest of the house and the family. For this, you need a space all your own, furniture (maybe with security locks), and equipment that fits the space that you have available. You will need a desk or one or more flat surfaces big enough to use for deskwork (such as making out invoices, paying bills, or taking phone orders).

You will also need a clean, flat, stable surface for your computer, printer, fax, copier, and scanner. You need to find a comfortable chair or stool. You may have one around the house that will work.

QUICK Tip

Add More Storage Room: You may need to store specialty phone books and technical manuals that come with computers and other equipment. Bookcases work well for these situations.

If you plan to have customers come into your home, you will need a clean, uncluttered place for them to wait or talk with you. Items to furnish this area will be high on your priority list, such as a simple chair, a lamp, and a small side table.

Alert!

Avoid Liability Problems: Having customers in your home may cause a liability problem. Check with your insurance agent to see if your home insurance policy covers injuries to and from customers. (More on insurance in Chapter 12.)

There are other things you may need for a particular business, like a postage meter, car, pager, etc. However, at the outset of your business, basic equipment, furniture, and supplies should be a top priority for you and your budget. If you want to consider other items, do so within the context of your priorities and your budget after you have arranged to meet your basic needs.

When deciding what equipment you need, ask some important questions. How big a space will you need? How much space is available or could be made available? If you have to move a lot of furniture, toys, or sporting equipment, where will it go? Is there enough space where you want to move things to? If you do not live alone, you may need to negotiate not only the amount of space you want to take up, but when you use the equipment in that space and when a family member uses it.

Home Office Equipment

The equipment of today's home-based business is vastly different than what it was several years ago. New technologies have changed the way people work and the tools they use to get their work done. (Review the checklist of items in Figure 3.2.) One advantage of the incredible technology available today is that it can greatly simplify running your business. It can make it possible for you to do many things independently that you once would have had to hire someone else to do for you. One disadvantage of that incredible technology is that it can seem like very complicated machinery when it malfunctions. This is especially true if you are not a *techie type*. Do not despair.

With the advances also comes choice. Whatever the piece of equipment, you can choose from hundreds of different models and features. Sifting through all the choices can seem to take forever, but taking the time to find what is right for you and your situation will be worth it in the end.

Alert!

Prevent Identity Theft: To prevent identity theft, use a shredder when you dispose of all paper that contains your personal identity information. Do the same with all business information you deem private, such as trade secrets, bank account numbers, credit cards, ID numbers, and income and expense figures.

Figure 3.2: CHECKLIST OF OFFICE EQUIPMENT AND SUPPLIES

Basic/Start-Up Equipment & Supplies:

☐ Computer
☐ Word-processing software
☐ Modem or DSL for Internet access
☐ Laser printer
☐ Computer cable, surge protector
☐ Paper for printer, one carton
☐ Letterhead
☐ Envelopes, box for correspondence
☐ Printed business cards
☐ Dozen 8½ x 11 lined writing pads
☐ Telephone
☐ Answering machine
☐ Work area (table, desk, or flat surface)
☐ Chair
☐ Accounting pads, 4 and 6 column
☐ Manila file folders, one box
☐ Paper clips (various sizes)
☐ Stapler and staples
☐ File cabinet
☐ Pens and pencils
☐ Ruler
☐ Scissors
☐ Shipping materials for product
☐ Postage stamps
☐ Shipping & postage labels

Optional Start-up Equipment & Supplies:

☐ Fax machine
☐ Small copier
☐ Scanner
☐ Post-It notes and flags
☐ Label maker
☐ Rolodex
☐ Tape recorder, small
☐ Presentation folders

Phone Lines

Many people who start a home business begin by using their home phone to place and receive business calls. There is a real downside to doing this. You may be giving up privacy and security. If your home phone number is listed in local phone books, church memberships, club memberships, or at your children's school—it is associated with your home address.

There are many reasons why you would not want your customers or your vendors to know where you live. Security and privacy are the primary reasons to keep your business and family somewhat separate. There is also the issue of children tying up your only phone line either talking or on the computer. So, if you can, get a separate phone line that is only used for your business.

QUICK Tip

Need for Additional Phone Lines: Ideally home businesses that need to access the Internet, send and receive faxes, and speak to customers on the phone should consider two lines dedicated to the businesses. With two lines, you can be working on the Internet and still take customer calls.

Parking

If customers or vendors will visit your home-based business regularly, that does not automatically mean you cannot run a home-based business. It only means that there are certain things to consider. You will want adequate parking nearby for the customers and vendors who come to your home.

If you live in the *snowbelt*, you will want to be able to rely on having the snow and ice cleared well enough to ensure safe places for parking and safe passage to your door.

Alert!

Parking Restrictions: Many cities have parking restrictions for snow removal to which you may need to alert your customers. Be sure to check with your local town authorities regarding any type of parking issue.

You will need to be aware of all parking laws in your city. Some neighborhoods restrict parking to residents. Some allow parking for the general public only during certain hours or only one side of the street. You may need to alert those with whom you do business in your home to the parking problems they will encounter and the solutions you can provide, such as a pass you get from the authorities that can be put on a dashboard.

If you have customers who use public transportation, you will want your home to be easily accessible by public transportation. Consider your customer base and potential customers who are disabled. You may need to make your home easily accessible for them.

You may be able to lease one or more parking spaces nearby from neighbors or other a commercial business operation on which you can put a sign that specifies parking only for your business.

Your home-based business may be near a public parking garage. If you are that lucky, let your customers and vendors know about the garage, where the entrance is located, and the approximate rates. You may also be able to strike a deal with the garage owner for discounts given to your visitors.

Whatever type of parking is available, keep watch that your visitors do not park illegally or block the driveway of a neighbor.

Chapter

A Home-Based Business and Your Family

Be prepared to deal with those little problems that families and friends bring into a home-based situation.

- ▶ **Family Support and Distractions**
- ▶ **Naysayers**
- ▶ **Friends and Neighbors**
- ▶ **Security**

Family Support and Distractions

Ask anyone who has a home-based business and he or she will tell you that the hardest thing to overcome when working from home is the interruptions and distractions. It is realistic to expect that you may need to cope with a toddler crying in the background when the little one needs to be fed or go down for a nap. On the day when you really need quiet to concentrate, your next door neighbor will remodel his garage or cut down a tree in his backyard.

QUICK Tip

Don't Be Too Comfortable At Home: Working at home has become the hottest trend for start-up businesses. However, some of the very reasons you may want to work at home can also turn out to be distractions, such as children, parents, or a spouse. Even the relaxed atmosphere of your home can offer you a million ways to avoid doing your work.

As for distractions, you may need to take your work to another part of the house or even outside your home. Do not hesitate to take your work outside. Bring it to a library or other quiet space. If you can afford it, hire child-care help or ask someone to watch your little one. Neighbors with small children may be able to help you, if you will help them at other times. Grandparents might be available to help out. Think about your circumstances; identify the distractions; and, devise a plan to help you cope with them as much as you can. When you cannot shake the distractions, you may just need to stop work and take a short break. Remember, that is one of the reasons you chose a home-based business—to set your own work schedule.

There are possible solutions. You can arrange your schedule around those things that you have control over. Do not have customers or vendors come during problematic times. Schedule conference calls at those times when family members are asleep or not around. Try to do paperwork and other things that require your undivided attention when you know that no one will be competing for it. Negotiate with friends and family on a time you can close a door and have a few minutes of quiet.

One of the greatest assets to your home business can be your family. Their support and loyalty can provide you the peace of mind to be a success. Win their support in your home-based business by involving them right at the beginning. Your spouse may be the biggest support of your business, both financially and by encouraging you to reach for your dream. Older children can be assigned more chores, minor business work, or used as a focus group to test your products. Younger children can be involved in making decisions, too, or at least asked for their opinion.

As for being a distraction, children and pets sometimes need immediate attention, no matter what their at-home parent is doing. Almost every at-home worker has had the experience of being on an important business phone call when the children begin to scream or the dog starts nonstop barking. We have all been through it.

Keep your cool and your humor. If there is a real emergency, excuse yourself and promise to return the call at a later time. For nonemergencies, rely on you sense of humor.

Alert!

Plan for Your Workspace: While it is possible to conduct your business from home and maintain a businesslike image, it can take some serious planning. You may have to make a few changes in your household routine and space. If possible, have your workplace close to the entrance. (The less of your home that a customer must walk through the better.)

Separate Entrance

Another thing to consider about your workspace is whether your business will have a separate entrance. If it will, keep that general area neat and safe. Post a sign that directs customers and vendors to the correct door.

If a separate entrance is a luxury that is not available to you, keep all areas free of clutter. If customers and vendors need to walk past your bedroom or through your kitchen to get to your workspace, have the dishes washed and put away and the dirty laundry out of sight. Keep the areas that customers and vendors will see clean, dusted, and tidied up. People connect what they see in your home with the quality of work you do.

Try to arrange your space, no matter how small, so that your customers will be comfortable doing business in your home. Customers need to feel comfortable working with you. Make sure there is enough space, furniture, light, and heat or air conditioning to allow them to feel comfortable so that they will work with you and refer others to you.

QUICK Tip

Be Creative When Identifying a Work Space: When you consider which spaces you can use for business activities, think about traffic patterns to and around your workspace. While a separate room or building is ideal, it is also possible to create a workspace with furniture or screens as room dividers.

As you look over your home and consider the possible spaces you can use for your business, imagine yourself there day after day in that space. You may need to weigh certain variables against each other. Do not dismiss the creature comforts as unimportant. If you are someone that absolutely needs daylight, a basement space may not be your best choice. Perhaps you would really like a separate room with a door, but the only possibility is space on the side of the house where you would struggle each day with the heat and intensity of the sun. If you cannot make the changes necessary to create space conducive to working comfortably (air conditioning, sun-blocking shades), you may be better off considering that alcove off the dining room, even if it does not have a door that you can close.

QUICK Tip

Conducting Business Outside: If you will conduct some or all of your business in a garden or outbuilding, such as a barn, greenhouse, or detached garage, be sure that walkways to your area have adequate signage to guide customers and vendors to the correct area. Keep the grass manicured, the sidewalks clear, and the snow and ice removed.

Naysayers

Deciding to open a home-based business may not get the reaction you were hoping for from your family and others. It could be because family finances are so tight that the loss of your salary will cause a real cutback. It could be because a family member may feel that you will not have any extra time for him or her. It could be a bit of jealously that you are able to do something that this person always wanted to do.

QUICK Tip

Deal with the Naysayers: Relax and deal with the naysayers. In business you may be forced to deal with difficult people or uncomfortable situations. Turn this potential challenge into a learning opportunity.

A naysayer may have legitimate concerns. It may be your spouse who is concerned about finances. It may be one of your children who is afraid that you won't be able to spend time playing together. It may be your parents who are concerned about your losing the employee benefits you currently have at your job.

With the material in this book and with your research into your home-based business, you will probably be able to show the naysayers that you know what you are doing and have planned for any problem. On the other hand, if the naysayer has a legitimate point that you haven't thought about, you may want to draft the naysayer into helping you figure out a solution.

Friends and Neighbors

Friends and neighbors can be your first and best customers, or they can be the worst naysayers. As with family, you probably want to enlist the help from your friends when you are first planning your home-based business. A good friend can be both a focus group and a part-time sales person for your product.

If your are quitting a job to open your home-based business, try to keep in contact with the friends you made at your previous job. They can also be sales people for your product.

Business Referrals: The majority of sales for home-based businesses comes from word of mouth referrals. Tell everyone about your product; they may pass on the information to a future customer.

If you are planning to quit a job in order to start a home-based business, you need to be very careful that your family can afford that loss of income. Ask yourself if there is money available to pay the standard household bills such as mortgage, utilities, food, and child care for the length of time until your business begins to make money. You may need to stay at your current job or work on a part-time basis until your home-based business starts bringing in profit. In most cases, profit does not come immediately and a home-based business may take years before it brings in a significant amount.

Alert!

Profit and Your Home-Based Business: Many home-based businesses do not show any profit in the first year. Some business experts say that on average it takes at least five years for a business to establish itself and show continuous profit.

It is not only a *lack of income*, but you also need to be aware of the *expense* in opening a business, plus the expenses that your family normally has. In the following chapters we will discuss the possible expenses of opening a home-based business. (Chapter 9 discusses budgets for both your family and your business. By creating a budget for both, you will be more able to determine if your family can afford a home-based business.)

Pay Current Obligations First: Bills for court-appointed child support, bankruptcy paybacks, court financial judgments, and student loans must be paid on time. If you ignore these bills, not only can your credit be affected, but you may find yourself in trouble with the legal system. Both of these could negatively affect your new business.

Security

There was a time when you could trust everyone and you could keep the doors unlocked. Sadly, that is no longer true. Security is a real concern. It becomes even more important when you become a business owner.

If you sell anything to the public using credit cards, you hold access to your customers' financial life. If you provide professional services (law, medical, financial), you probably hold many of your customers' secrets. Face it, there are nasty people out there that would love to get this type of information about your customers. Unfortunately, there are also people who enjoy targeting business owners because of the myth that business owners are financially well-off. The security issue is not just for business records and money, it is also for your family.

SECTION II:

Start Getting Organized

Chapter

Prioritize Your Ideas

No matter the kind of home-based business you are starting, you need to use your time wisely—your time both as a business owner and as a person.

▶ **Your Time is Valuable**

▶ **Choose a Business You Can Grow to Love**

▶ **Identify Your Goals**

▶ **Create a Daily Activity List**

▶ **Analyze Your Activity List**

▶ **Focus Your Initiative**

▶ **Identify Your Business Skills**

▶ **Know Your Personal Limitations**

▶ **Develop Balance in Your Life**

Your Time is Valuable

It is easy to fall into the old-fashioned perception that work done from home is much less important than the same job done in an office. You hear yourself called housewife, househusband, or even Mr. Mom just because you are the person who is always at home. You may even find yourself volunteered to do lots of things that retired or stay-at-home spouses do, because everyone knows you are always at home.

How you deal with this depends on the goals for your business. If your at-home business is a stepping stone to that time when the business grows into its own office, you may want to let everyone know the hours you are available for nonbusiness issues. There is nothing wrong with saying to chatty family and friends that you will call them back after business hours. (In our experience, caller ID is one of the greatest tools for controlling time.)

If your business goals are smaller (but certainly not less important) and you want to work at home in order to enjoy the family chores while making money, let that be known, too. It is great to know that one member of the family can take in packages, pick up sick kids at school, and keep up with the chores. If this describes you, be watchful of two things. First, do not neglect the business once you have started it. Second, do not let the rest of the family take advantage of your time. In order to use precious time wisely, the home-based business owner needs to *manage* it. The following activities will help.

Choose a Business You Can Grow to Love

You become passionate about your work if you like that you will work at home and you like the mission you choose for your home-based business. Whether your mission comes from a long cherished dream or straight out of the Yellow Pages, you truly should choose a business that you feel you could grow to love. When you think about what it is you want to have for a mission, you will be able to develop a passion for it if you feel delighted when you think of your product or service as being something people really need or want and you are the lucky one to be able to provide it. If you wax enthusiastic to others when you describe what you want to do for a living, you have passion. Moreover, when no one is around to listen, if you feel so good about it that you can honestly say to yourself *this is great*, then you have the passion it takes to be a success.

Identify Your Goals

The first step towards successful time management is to define what your personal and business goals are. Be precise. Think about what you want to accomplish in your life and in your business. Then write them down on paper. Do not overstate what you truly believe you can achieve given your skills, abilities, family situation, financial needs and plans, and workspace.

Rate your goals as short-term, intermediate, or, long-term. Short-term goals are things to do today, next week, or next month. Intermediate goals usually are met on a quarterly basis and do not extend beyond three years. Long-term goals are usually expressed in five-year increments.

Short-Term Goals

Short-term goals are usually expressed as what you need to accomplish each day, week, and month. Goals that are framed around these time divisions enable you to set realistic priorities and design appropriate activities. Keep track of these goals by using a business calendar.

Intermediate Goals

For your home-based business, intermediate goals are usually objectives that come up monthly, quarterly, or by season. The federal tax year and government reporting requirements are usually expressed as quarterly time periods. (Many industries are based on calendar quarters.)

Another intermediate time period revolves around holidays. If your home-based business produces holiday-oriented items or sells more before certain holidays, your intermediate goals should be set by the holidays in a year.

Still another way to set intermediate goals is by seasons. Farmers set their intermediate goals so that they can be prepared for the activities done in each season. Intermediate goals allow you to stay flexible and adjust your schedule as necessary with the least amount of stress.

Long-Term Goals

Long-term goals are your dreams, your wants, what you are working toward. Writing down your long-term goals not only gives you something to attain, it puts all the hard work of a home-based business into focus.

CASE STUDY: Goals for a Home-Based Seasonal Cookie Business

PERSONAL GOALS

   Short-term:
      This month—paint the kitchen
      Next month—buy Mom's birthday present
   Intermediate:
      Spring—till flower beds, plant seeds
      Summer—buy daffodil bulbs
      Fall—plant bulbs
      Winter—cover roses
   Long-term:
      Fifteen years—have all children in college

BUSINESS GOALS

   Short-term:
      This week—finish business proposal
      Next week—send out mailing to local businesses
   Intermediate:
      January—take orders and make Valentine's Day items
      February—deliver Valentine's Day items
      March—take orders and make Easter/Spring items
      April—deliver Easter/Spring items, orders for Mom's Day
      May—deliver Mom's Day items
      June—take orders and make July 4th items
      July—deliver July 4th items
      August—take orders and make back to school items
      September—deliver back-to-school items, take orders for Halloween, Thanksgiving, Christmas, and New Years items.
   Long-term:
      Five years—pay back start-up loans; hire employees
      Ten years—move home-based business to its own building

Reevaluate Your Goals

As your business progresses, set time aside to contemplate your many goals. Evaluate them; stick to them or change them; rearrange them; and, otherwise deal with the reality of your business and personal life choices. The end of each month is a good time to do this.

Create a Daily Activity List

To help you decide on the amount of time available in your daily life to launch your business, you first need to assemble two pieces of information.

1. What tasks do you need to spend your time on?
2. What is the length of time you use for each activity?

Take a long, hard, detailed look at the demands on your time. Review your life's activities for at least a week. If a two-week time frame fits better with your lifestyle, make your review for that duration. At the end of each day, over the period of time you choose to review, identify, and record every activity. Estimate (as close as you can) the exact amount of time you devoted to each one. Figure 5.1 is a list of general activities you may want to include. Add more categories as fits your specific situation.

When you have finished estimating the time you use for each activity in each of your categories, add up the time you spend each day. It should come within a few minutes of twenty-four hours.

Figure 5.1: DAILY ACTIVITIES THAT TAKE A DEMAND ON YOUR TIME

- sleep
- shopping
- grooming
- travel and transportation
- child care
- time on all jobs you have outside the home
- medical matters
- exercise
- housework
- volunteer work
- cooking
- hobbies
- eating
- socializing with family
- social meetings
- socializing with friends
- time you feel you waste

Alert!

Do Not Make Judgments, Now: As you prepare your daily activities list, do not make judgments about whether you should or should not do an activity. Do not concern yourself with cutting back on specific time allotments.

Analyze Your Activity List

The purpose of analyzing your activity list is to identify the extra time you will need to fit running a home-based business into your life without diminishing the important activities or diminishing the quality of your life. You are going to analyze each activity's significance to you and your family. Get input from family members about their views of what is significant to them. Prepare to make your value judgments by doing four things.

1. Look at your business and personal goals.
2. Complete your daily activity list.
3. Think about how your daily activities and your personal goals mesh or are in conflict. Determine if these activities might be affected by your business goals. Think about the needs of your family and which activities are important to them.
4. Label each personal activity.
    - C = continue spending the same amount of time
    - M = modify or change the activity
    - L = spend less time doing the activity
    - D = delegate the activity to someone else or draw a line through the activity you will eliminate

- C *activities* are those that you decide you must keep on using the same amount of time for, no matter what. It will be a rare day in your life when you do not use the same amount of time for these activities. For example, "C" would be alongside the amount of sleep you must have.
- M *activities* are those that can modified. For example, you may conclude that you would be able to change the time of your exercise from one part of the day to another.

- *L activities* are ones that you need to be careful about reducing. Some people can get by with less time for eating or sleeping—most cannot. The time you use for being with friends or participating in recreation may need to be realigned, not necessarily shrunk. Can you explain to your friend what your new venture is all about and negotiate a weekly tennis game to another day of the week?
- *D activities* are those that you ask others to share. Ask family members to take over some chores. Be sure they are ones that you know they have the capacity to learn and do. If they do not know how to do what you ask, teach them. Supervise them, as appropriate. Refrain from meddling. It causes strife and can become a counterproductive use of time. Get progress reports from them along the way and at the end. Ask if they need help to complete the task if they are stressed. Otherwise, let them complete what you have asked.

When you get to Chapter 6, use the results of these steps to determine the amount of time that you can allot to your business start-up activities. You can expect that the start-up phase will be time-intensive. Consequently, you may change your mind about the amount of time you apportion to various personal activities.

Focus Your Initiative

To acquire initiative, practice thinking and acting independently. Set your alarm to get up a half hour early each morning for seven days straight. Get up and get out of bed right away. No matter what the situation, if you can do this, you can develop the quality of initiative. This little exercise can reveal to yourself that you can get the upper hand over yourself. If you can get the upper hand over yourself, you can gain it over your business.

Initiative is a function of your self-confidence. It requires you to get yourself up to the point in which you have a feeling that you are inventive or creative and that you can tackle what you must. Put it in your head that you are ready whenever you need to be. When you run your own business, no one will be waiting for you to sign in or punch a time clock.

You can gain the initiative to decide where you are going and how you are going to get there by preparing your business plan. Your plan and the decisions you make about what you are going to do will enable you to be able to take the initiative necessary for you to succeed. It is the actual process of making the plan yourself, not using a cookie-cutter one you find in a book or on the Internet, that will help you develop initiative.

Commit to Working Hard

If you have decided to start a home-based business, you must have made the commitment to work hard. However, there are several ways that hard work can be made less formidable. Break down tasks into one or more sections you can accomplish over the time period you allocate. Work all the hours you need to accomplish your priorities for each day. Maintain your mental and physical health, so that you have the capacity to work with the intensity demanded of you.

Alert!

Upsides and Downsides: One of the upsides of having a home-based business is that you can take a few minutes each hour or whenever you want to for a quick little break from the intensity of your activities. One of downsides is that you must minimize dealing with family and friends during the time you set aside to work.

Keep distractions and interruptions to a minimum. Limit nonwork activities during your work time. Keep anxiety down by being honest with yourself about your skills, knowledge, and abilities.

Be Optimistic

When things go wrong, the natural feelings of despair and disappointment that most feel can quickly take hold and damage the chance of a home-based business' success. To learn how to move past the bad times and generate optimism, the tool you need is to have a realistic, well-thought-out business plan that you stick to. A plan lets you know you are right where you should be, or that if you make certain changes in your plan, you will to be able to get where you want to go.

Be Prepared

Being able to prepare is a practical skill for home-based business owners. Learn to be prepared by seeing to it that you have enough work and office space, enough inventory to meet customers' needs, and enough money to pay bills. Do comprehensive research before you buy equipment. You can be prepared by having enough of the right help to accomplish a project, enough time to devote to marketing and sales, enough planning, or any other activity that is part of the business. You can be prepared by anticipating an upturn or downturn in your market.

Identify Your Business Skills

A major ingredient a small business needs to survive and thrive is its owner's management skills. These skills include financial management, making decisions, running operations, marketing, sales, planning, gathering data, goal setting, creative problem solving, and personnel skills.

If you do not yet have all the essential business skills, there are several ways to learn them. You may have learned some of these skills as an employee, as a volunteer, or as a homemaker. If you identify a skill you need, perhaps you can work for a while in the industry or type of business you want to start. Another way to learn is to take classes at a local business school, community college, or on the Internet. Figure 5.2 lists some basic decision-making steps that you will need to make use of in your new business.

Figure 5.2: BUSINESS DECISION-MAKING—STEP-BY-STEP

- Know when you have a problem.
- Figure out what the solution needs to accomplish.
- Analyze the situation.
- Identify the major uncertainties.
- Determine potential solutions and brainstorm alternatives.
- Gather data.
- Analyze which alternative might work best given the specific problem and your particular situation.
- Select the alternative that seems most likely to work.
- Devise an action plan you can implement.
- Implement the plan.
- Follow up to see how the decision worked and evaluate its effectiveness in solving the problem.

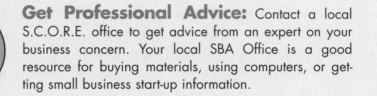 **Get Professional Advice:** Contact a local S.C.O.R.E. office to get advice from an expert on your business concern. Your local SBA Office is a good resource for buying materials, using computers, or getting small business start-up information.

Know Your Personal Limitations

In your business, learn to know yourself by determining which tasks you can do well, which you cannot, and which ones you cannot do at all. Identify what tasks you do not want to do. Make a plan for what to do when you cannot do something. Few people can perform all the functions necessary to run a business, no matter how small the business.

Whether you run a manufacturing company that employs one hundred people or operate out of a tiny home-based office or shop, you will need to know when to get help. Maybe you will have to hire someone to come in to help with child care or housework. Perhaps getting help means hiring more employees or finding an accountant to do your taxes. If a need goes unmet, it can spell trouble for your business. Do not let false pride get in your way. Put it into your head to get the help you need when you need it.

Develop Balance in Your Life

There are benefits of putting yourself on a schedule. A schedule is your timetable—a plan for the use of your time. A well-thought-out and implemented schedule should never be something that constricts you. It should have the opposite effect—it should free you and enable you to achieve your goal.

Make your schedule thorough, keep it current and sensible, and apply it with flexibility. It lets you accept that you may have to change plans at any time and in midstream to meet your goals. Do not schedule yourself back-to-back throughout the day. Leave some *wiggle room* in your schedule so you can handle the unexpected—add appointments, reschedule important ones, or seize an opportunity you did not anticipate.

Your physical needs such as your health, wellness, and everyday activities of living deserve place in your written schedule. Lack of attention to your personal health can result in a major source of tension for you and therefore hamper you in your business.

Personal Schedule

Identify the amount of time you need to devote to sleep. It is tempting to short yourself in this area. This is acceptable once in awhile, like when you bring your baby home from the hospital or absolutely have to make a deadline. However, as a habit, research shows that humans do not function optimally if they do not have eight hours each day.

You may want to plan for a year's worth of dental, medical, and other health care appointments. Many medical offices let you schedule a year ahead of time. If not, put a reminder in your calendar when you have to call to make an appointment.

Set aside time in your schedule to exercise. You may want to block off one hour each day to do aerobics or Pilates or weight training. You may prefer to tuck shorter periods of exercise into several spots in your day. You can take a five-minute break each hour and do some stretching or strength training. If you get your exercise gardening or playing sports, let your schedule reflect that.

Settle on what the basic chores and survival tasks are in your life and locate opportunities in your schedule to do them. Give yourself opportunities in your schedule to fulfill your intellectual, cultural, and aesthetic needs. You may enjoy something as simple as listening to your favorite CD, reading a novel, or doing some knitting or a similar, almost automatic activity.

Social Schedule

Personal relationships are noted here only within the context of demands upon your time and because you need to budget relationship management activities in your schedule. For example, your children or grandchildren may need to have you at school functions, supervise their play, or attend their sporting events. Find out when and where such events will take place, what your role will be, and note such details in your calendar of scheduled events.

Because whomever you share your life with is deserving of your attention and participation, you need to consider dates and times special to them that you need to honor, as much as they need to do the same for you. Perhaps it is as simple as sharing one or more meals each day, or perhaps it is as complex as attending a family reunion. If you cannot keep a scheduled commitment, work it out with those affected.

Your job is to work with your family to identify those times and put them into your schedule while at the same time teaching them about your time needs in your new business. Your life can be much less stressful if you are able to look at your calendar and explain honestly to a customer, friend, or family member that you already have a prior commitment at a time they are pressuring you to do something else. When problems with work arise, consult your calendar and negotiate with your family and customers any last minute changes you need to make in your time with them.

QUICK Tip

Use Your Schedule as a Tool: A written schedule is a tool that will allow you to reap one of the major benefits of having a home-based business—doing things in your own time.

Chapter

Use Your Time, Wisely

In order to work efficiently, you must identify the tasks that need to be done; prioritize the tasks; then be sure to complete the most important tasks first.

- ▶ **Prioritize Your Tasks**
- ▶ **Plan Your Time**
- ▶ **Too Much Work and Not Enough Time**
- ▶ **Control Your Interruptions**
- ▶ **Project-Scheduling Challenges**
- ▶ **Inventory-Scheduling Challenges**

Prioritize Your Tasks

There is a sure way to be satisfied about your work at the end of each day. Do only that which is important. If you end each day knowing you worked only on what you believe is important, you can attain a feeling of contentment— no matter how hectic your life. To determine what *important* means to you, prioritize your tasks. Although there are many different approaches to prioritizing, the most useful is to think in three levels of priorities. (More than three levels and planning your time can become an unwieldy problem.)

Begin by assigning different levels of priorities to your various tasks. There will be things you do on most days, such as check your email. You are likely to experience critical, urgent, and vital tasks. Some of these will be expected, some unexpected. Sometimes routine tasks become urgent.

Next, categorize tasks. One way to do this is to fit each one into one of three groups labeled A, B, C or 1, 2, 3, with the labels reflecting:

A. Must do today.

B. Would like to do today.

C. Only do today if all of the tasks in the other two categories are already done.

QUICK Tip

Create To-Do Lists:

1. Daily to-do items. Include everything you need to do each day.
2. Weekly to-do items. This list should be your basic date book of routine events such as meetings or classes.
3. Monthly to-do items. Include things you want to handle on a regular basis, but not necessarily as a daily routine. These could be tasks such as taking inventory, ordering special materials, or doing market research.

Keep the daily to-do list in front of you (on paper or on your computer) with the items marked in order of their importance. Carry it with you so you can have instant access to it if you go outside the home to work on your business. After you mark an item with a priority, allocate the amount of time you plan to spend on it.

At the start of your day, begin to work on the task you have labeled as most important. If you finish it, then get to work on the next important item (which has then become your *new*, most important one). Again, work on that task until you finish it. Then cross it off and start on the next one.

If you are interrupted while you work, you have a decision to make—is responding to the interruption more or less important to you than continuing with your work? Of course, emergencies do arise. If you choose to handle the interruption or the emergency, you have just given yourself a new priority. That can be fine. However, realize that your decision to handle a new matter rearranged your priorities. So work on the new matter until you complete it. Then, at the end of each day, you will have the satisfaction of knowing that you used your time to work on the most important priorities you have.

Multitasking

The key to multitasking is to know what tasks can be combined for efficiency's sake without sacrificing quality in the performance of those tasks. If you schedule a business meeting over lunch, you can have a healthy lunch while discussing business matters with your lunch guest. Business lunches are not limited to clients. If you and your business partner cannot ever seem to keep your appointment to discuss long-range business planning, perhaps a lunch date is the answer.

Delegating to Others

To save time, business owners need to be able to delegate. Moreover, they have to do it appropriately or face negative consequences. When you are about to be hit with three deadlines simultaneously, it may be time to delegate. If you find that you are rewriting your to-do list over onto the next day and the next day, your time is being lost without achieving your goals. Look for ways to delegate. If you choose the right employees, partners, or collaborators, delegating will be easy and successful.

Networking

One of the best practical ways to use your time is when you network. Networking is important because it is the best marketing—word-of-mouth.

Incorporate networking into your planned use of time. Give it adequate space on your calendar.

Plan Your Time

A calendar is a great device to help you keep yourself abreast of your plans. Make it one that you keep with ease and that reflects your priorities. Conceive of it as your personalized tool that enables you to budget your finite resource of time.

Calendars are not for everyone. Some people are able to keep to their schedules, list their priorities, make out a to-do list, and work from there. They choose not to use a calendar because timelines are not relevant to their business or personal situation.

However, for those of us who need to account for deadlines, appointments, meetings, vendors, customers, inventories, colleagues, and complicated family situations, calendars are an indispensable tool. At the end of each day or the very first thing at the start of your business day, review what you have scheduled into your calendar. Establish your priorities for the day and allocate time for each. Write your to-do list. (Be aware that you may have to adapt your day to meet unforeseen happenings.)

You may want to use an hour-by-hour, day-by-day, and week-by-week calendar that keeps track of your obligations. This style of calendar lets you allocate your time quite specifically. It can provide you with a handy reference and clear guideline of all tasks that you must do and when you must do them. This approach dovetails nicely if you prepare a list of your priorities and to-do list for each day and each week. It lets you measure at a glance how you are doing with accomplishing your responsibilities.

Keep Two Calendars—One Big, One Small

Put a big calendar that shows the entire month on your workspace or wall. Use a small calendar that lets you enter appointment times, deadlines, and notes. Keep the smaller calendar with you at all times to record both personal and business commitments. It is an excellent tool to use to prevent yourself from creating scheduling conflicts.

QUICK Tip

Use a Computer Calendar: You may also want to use computer calendars. Computer calendars installed in Windows Microsoft Works and other software programs have calendars that you can use on your desktop or laptop computer to record each appointment, event, and holiday. Many have features that allow your computer to remind you of dates and times.

Alert!

Backup Electronic Data: If you enter any information into a desktop computer, cell phone, or palm-sized computer, be sure that you frequently backup and save the information in case you lose the electronic version.

Too Much Work and Not Enough Time

If you seem to have too much to do, there are several things you may be able to do to alleviate the problem. Call your customer and negotiate a new deadline. Subcontract some or all of the work to someone you trust and who can do the work within the time frame you must meet. If you want to accept a new customer but the project will consume too much time in your schedule, see if you can negotiate a timeline you can honestly meet.

Another option to any scheduling problem is to just say no. However, saying no can be an expensive decision. It can be emotionally difficult when you face the consequences of saying no. Your best choice of action is to look at your calendar and calculate what free time you have and do not have. Say yes or no based upon your priorities and goals. Then, you can live with your decision knowing that you made the best choice under the circumstances.

Control Your Interruptions

Relaxation techniques and just plain fun are essential in everyone's life. However, they can get out of control and gobble up precious time that you need to use for your business or personal obligations. The solution is to put limits on the time you use to relax. The key is to budget time for your favorite pursuits without wasting time. Be honest with yourself about the amount of time you can allow for them so that you do not take away time from your business and family responsibilities.

When you lose your concentration, take a break. Do some stretching. Take the dog for a walk around the block. Work on another task for a short time until you feel you can regain your concentration on the one you abandoned. The length of your break depends upon the amount of time you can afford in your schedule and the time it will take for you to be refreshed enough to resume working on your priority.

Meetings

If you attend meetings as part of your business, the best ways for you to save time is to:

- meet only when necessary;
- keep meetings as brief as possible;
- follow an agenda with specific time allocated for each topic;
- stay focused on the matters under discussion;
- facilitate people's participation as those who do not participate can use up your time telling you later on what they wanted to say when you met;
- strive to have as many decisions made at the meeting as possible, and identify undecided matters and the process to be used to get decisions made; and,
- avoid interruptions by getting the attendees to agree at the outset to turn cell phones off, use the vibrating ring, and take critical calls outside the meeting space.

Your time is precious. Other people think their time is precious and will appreciate your willingness to conserve it.

Telephone Interruptions

The telephone can be critical to your existence, but it can be a pesky time management problem. When you are busy and the phone rings, do you answer it? Before the phone starts to ring for the day, look at your priorities, make out your to-do list, and decide if you will answer the phone today. When it does ring, how important is it to you to continue working on your priority? It might be the call you have been waiting for from a good customer. It might be a call from a loved one in trouble. If you have caller ID, you have help to answer that question. It might be a number you do not know, so it could be a potential customer.

Weigh your potential loss of time with the consequences of not answering and decide what you want to do. When you decide that you cannot afford an interruption, do not answer the phone. You have the option to turn off the ringing mechanism. You can let it go on the answering machine then return the call later that day when you can. If you are talking with someone who is eating up the time you need to devote to a task or meeting, be firm, polite, and explain you why you have to hang up. You can ask if you can call the person back when the crunch is past and you are free.

Alert!

Return Customer Phone Calls, Promptly: Returning customer and potential customer phone calls is important in every business. Make it a policy to return phone calls within twenty-four hours during the week and Monday morning for weekend calls.

Use the phone to help you conserve time. For example, use a conference call for local and long-distance meetings. Price it out based on your travel time and costs. Calculate if it will be less time consuming and less expensive than being there in person.

Computer Interruptions

Email can gobble up time. There are simple steps you can take to deal with it during your workday. One way is not to rush to check it first thing in the morning. Instead, set your priorities for the day, then decide when handling it fits into your day's schedule. Check to see if you have received a message you are expecting and ignore the others until you have more time available.

However, do schedule in that time so you can reply, save, or delete each message on the day received.

If you are working online, your can turn off the notification that you have mail. If you have more than a half dozen sentences to communicate, it probably is worth creating a document that you send as an attachment. To reply to a message, use only the subject line to send simple communiqués, such as *thank you*. When you send a message, use only the subject line, such as "see you at Johnson's for lunch, 1 p.m." If you have a disagreement with someone, use the phone to resolve it.

Clerical Interruptions

The way to keep snail mail from taking up unnecessary time is to open it and process it on the day you receive it. Choose a place in your daily or weekly schedule when it is most convenient for you to dispose of your mail. Piles of unread, unanswered mail can get in the way of efficiency, however, the unhappy consequences of not paying bills on time or missed opportunities can also be problematic.

To minimize the amount of time you have to devote in your schedule to filing, handle each correspondence on the day received, but definitely as soon as your schedule will allow. Then file it.

Procrastination

Procrastination steals time more easily and cruelly than even long commutes and stacks of old papers past due for filing. If you find yourself putting things off until tomorrow and the next day and the next week, meet this habit head-on by using your schedule. Reexamine your goals, priorities, and calendar. When you are tempted to postpone or not do something, look at your schedule. What does it reveal about the consequences to your goals if you procrastinate?

Your schedule can help you decide whether you should negotiate a new deadline, reschedule a meeting, move back a product launch, or postpone delivery of an item or service. Check your goals to be sure that they are realistic. Revamp them if necessary to bring truth to your business operations and allow yourself to banish the urge to procrastinate.

Avoid routinely managing your time by crisis. Do not wait until things are on fire and you have to drop everything else to give time to a crisis. Instead, plan your work based on your priorities, with an eye to being flexible. You will thus minimize the opportunity for crises to happen and be better able to deal with them when they do occur.

QUICK Tip

Rearrange Your Plans: If you find yourself doing a bit of this and that but not accomplishing anything, review your priorities. Rearrange your plans in order to maximize the time you have to handle those tasks that must be accomplished.

Project-Scheduling Challenges

To help manage your time if your business is project driven, incorporate project-driven deadlines in your schedule by first entering on your calendar the date the project ends. Then work backwards from that date to insert each target date along the way. (This technique also works well for inventory management.)

Inventory-Scheduling Challenges

If you have inventory to manage, there are software programs that can help you keep track of critical dates that require you take action. It can alert you to when levels of each item needs to be reordered, becomes outdated, or is not moving as expected. Put a note in your calendars to alert you when to take action on your inventory needs.

SECTION III:

Develop Your Plans

Chapter

Make a Business Plan

Planning is the key to a successful home-based business. You may think your company is too small to use these professional tools, but every business, no matter the size, can benefit from strategic planning.

Start-Up Action Plan

A start-up action plan allows you to see all the tasks you must accomplish before your business is operational. To build your plan, work backward from the date you plan to have as your first day that you actually do business. (Figure 7.1 is a list of tasks you might consider for your action plan.)

The easiest way to create this plan is on a lined piece of paper. On the right side, write down all the actions or tasks that you must absolutely have done before opening day. Next to each task, write the date by when you want to have each step completed.

Figure 7.1: POTENTIAL TASKS FOR YOUR ACTION PLAN

- Discuss plans with your family.

- Find a space to do your work.

- Ask what kind of lead time the phone company needs to add features to your service.

- Determine the start date for electricity or gas.

- Determine if you need a license, different zoning, or other business permit. (If you do need permits, etc., ask how long it will take to get them.)

- Find an accountant, a lawyer, and any other necessary professional and technical help.

- Choose a name.

- Incorporate or set up some other form of legal entity.

- Determine the office equipment and office supplies you need.

- Identify the necessary furniture.

- Determine the necessary amount of inventory or manufacturing supplies and when they need to arrive.

- Find vendors and negotiate contracts with each.

- Locate financing for your business.

- Choose an opening date.

Figure 7.1 does not list everything that you will need to put into a start-up plan, but it will help to start the process.

CASE STUDY: Producing T-Shirts on Time

If you want to sell the embroidered T-shirts you make beginning January 1st, you will want to have all of your tasks fully completed by November 30th. This date will allow you a cushion for things to go wrong. Under this plan, you will want to have the entire number of T-shirts you intend to sell embroidered by an early enough date to allow for problems—perhaps November 1st. To accomplish that, set a date by which you must order enough T-shirts and yarn from your vendors to have them on hand for you to embroider. (You will need to know how long it takes you to embroider each T-shirt.) You will also need to factor the time you use for all other business start-up activities, as well as your personal lifestyle demands.

The Importance of a Business Plan

The importance of having a business plan cannot be overstated, as much of your success depends upon it. Your business plan covers such things as funding, credit from suppliers, management of your operation and finances, and promotion and marketing of your business. The creation of a complete business plan shows whether your new venture has the potential to make a profit.

Whether you reach your goals and objectives will depend greatly upon what you put into your plan and how you implement it. It is the *key tool* to help you turn your dream into reality. It will help you examine the real world and then decide what is possible; when it is possible; and, how you have to structure your activities and funding to make it happen.

Developing a Business Plan

A business plan is a document that provides some key information for others and outlines what it is you hope to accomplish. One of its main benefits is that it forces you to look at what it is you think you want to do. It will help you determine if your idea is possible, or realize that it is not going to work. This process starts with asking yourself some core questions, then breaking down those questions with even more detailed analysis.

Before you begin writing your business plan, consider these five core questions.

1. What service or product do you want to have your business provide and what needs in the marketplace does it fill?
2. Who are the potential customers for your product or service and why will they purchase it from you?
3. How will you reach your potential customers?
4. What assistance will you need?
5. How much money (for both personal and business reasons) will you need to get off the ground and where will you get the financial resources to start your business?

Writing a Business Plan

Once you have done your research, you need to put it in writing. This section lays out one type of structure and format you can use. Review Figure 7.2 as you begin to write your business plan.

Figure 7.2: FOCUS ON YOUR BUSINESS PLAN

Keep these five things in mind as you begin writing your plan.

1. Keep only topics appropriate for your business. (You do not have to use all of the standard business plan topics.)

2. Make sure all entries are accurate. (Even if you decide to do an abbreviated or shortened business plan, this is not the place to fudge.)

3. Spend the most research time on marketing, cash flow, and the break-even point. These three topics will require more work than others.

4. Research and analysis of the data help to make the best business plans for home-based businesses.

5. Write your business plan for its reader, especially if you are using the plan to obtain funding.

The Time Period Your Plan Should Cover

The plan for your new business should cover at least a period of one year. For some businesses, plans typically cover three to five years. If you plan to seek a loan from a bank or other financial institution, the loan officer may ask you for a business plan that encompasses three to five years of activities.

QUICK Tip

Change is Constant: Flexibility in a home-based business owner is even more important than in many other business settings. When you make a change in your business plan, you may need to notify financial backers if the changes are substantially different from the business plan you used to obtain the loan.

Standard Business Plan Format

Most business plans begin with a cover sheet listing the company's name and the date the plan was written. Business plans usually have a table of contents that lists major subject headings and the page where each topic begins.

In addition to the cover page and table of contents, the following topics are common in business plans.

1. Summary Statement
2. Company Analysis
3. Your Product or Service
4. Industry Analysis
5. Market Analysis and Strategy
6. Management Analysis
7. Ownership
8. Expansion Goals
9. Financial Analysis
10. Schedule of Implementation

1. Summary Statement

The *summary statement* is a brief description of your business and the key elements in the business plan. (Figure 7.3 gives examples of possible topics and wording for your summary.) It is usually no longer than one page. The goal of the summary is to entice the reader to want to read the whole document.

Figure 7.3: SAMPLE INFORMATION FOR YOUR SUMMARY

Your summary may be like one of the following examples.

• Service or Product—Example: We will sell custom-made baskets.

• Target Market/Market Need—Example: We will serve interior decorators in the city that have no local source for these types of baskets.

• Competition—Example: We will compete with the large box stores who sell imports.

• Expertise and Skills—Example: We will be the only domestic basket maker in the county to have learned our craft abroad.

• Business Goals—Example: In three years we will capture 30% of the market.

• Existing Financial Picture—Example: We currently have a balance of $5,000 in an interest-bearing checking account with The Main Street Bank. Other business assets include $500 of appraised inventory and office equipment worth $1,000. We are asking for a business loan of $10,000 in order to supplement our inventory in preparation for a media-advertising blitz. (Use this when you are seeking a business loan.)

---

2. Company Analysis

The information provided in the company analysis section gives the reader an overview of your business-to-be. This includes a general description of your product or service, the business format, marketing plans, how you will operate the business, and the goals of the business. (You can include your thoughts on future expansion and incorporate the reasons you have chosen this type of business.)

3. Product or Service

Develop a detailed description of what you make or provide. Include your sales projections, any product evaluations that you think will help the reader understand your business, and a comparison of your service or products with your competitors' services, products, or product lines. (Be sure to describe the competitive advantages you will have over other producers, such as higher quality, uniqueness, location, credentials, or experience. Mention all things that set you apart from the competition and make you a better choice for your target market.)

4. Industry Analysis

The industry analysis usually begins with a description of your industry, trade, or profession. Define it. Give a short explanation of when the industry began; where it is today; and, what the general projections for industry growth are for the next five years.

CASE STUDY: Industry Analysis for the Pottery Maker

Lead-free clay potterymakers supply ¾ of all handcrafted pottery for use in schools. There are 8,383 schools in this state that buy $1,000,000 of lead-free pottery each year. There will be 210 new schools built in this state in the next five years. Combined with breakage at existing schools, this will increase demand for our product by 165% in the next three years.

---

5. Market Analysis and Strategy

The market analysis and strategy is an explanation of your potential base of customers, your competition, and your advertising program. Describe your target market in detail. Include features of your average customer such as age, geographic area, income, buying habits, etc. Identify the target market needs of your service or product. Give specific estimates as to the number of sales you expect. In this section, you will also want to describe the competition, how you compare with your competitors' service, product, price, location, etc.

Finally, detail how you intend to market your product of service. Describe your plans for websites, professional or trade associations, word-of-mouth, radio spots, cold calls, newspaper ads, networking opportunities, community bulletin boards, and magazines—and indicate how these will be effective for your message.

6. Management Analysis

The management analysis section should contain your résumé, your business experience, and the same for any employees or partners.

7. Ownership

The ownership section should contain a résumé and history of business experience for you and for any partners or part owners of the company. In this section you should also list the legal status of the business, such as "Incorporated in the State of Georgia," "sole proprietorship in the State of Illinois," "legal partnership in the State of Utah." In addition, you should attach copies of any legal incorporation papers, partnership agreements, or other legal documents about the business.

8. Expansion Goals

The expansion goals section describes where you want your business to be in three to five years. Also insert an explanation of how you will measure your operation. (Your readers will be interested in how you measure success for your plans. You can use dollars, units produced, units sold, number of clients, or any other system that measures your business' performance.) When you discuss any expansion plan, demonstrate that you will make decisions to expand based upon the realistic assessment of your past performance. (This gives confidence to the reader that you are a serious businessperson, intent on running a smart operation.)

9. Financial Analysis

In the financial analysis section, estimate the amount of capital you have to work with and its source. Insert your business budget, estimates for sales, expenses, and profit. Indicate the minimum profit you have to make in order for your expenses to be covered by your income.

10. Schedule of Implementation

The schedule of implementation section demonstrates that you have a solid grasp on the actions necessary to set up and run a business out of your home. Lay out timetables that list the action steps you plan to take. For example:

- If you will have inventory, show when you will order items, when you expect delivery, and when you will take your first order or make your first sale or delivery.
- If you are in a service profession, show when you graduated from school and when you will have all the licenses and credentials that you need to perform your service.
- If you need to remodel a space in your home, give the date when the work will be done and how soon after that you will be able to open for business.

QUICK Tip

Supporting Documents: Most business plans also include supporting documents such as tax returns, financial statements, bank statements and other information. These things may not be required for a home-based business.

Presenting Your Business Plan

You may find yourself in a position where you need to present your business plan to one or more people. The most common situation for this type of presentation is when you are asking for a business loan. However, you may also be called upon to present your plan in a professional networking event, to young people at a career day, to a potential landlord, or as part of an advertising event. Remember, the presentation is not just reading your business plan, it is talking about your plan, your business, and your view of where your business is headed in the future.

Your initial step is to determine your audience. Your presentation of your business plan will differ depending upon the audience. For example, if you are presenting your plan to a group of business people such as bankers or venture capitalists, the physical look of your business plan and your verbal presentation should be formal and businesslike.

Formal Business Presentations

A formal business plan is usually in a dark colored presentation binder. It should contain a title page with the name of your business in the center and your name, address, and phone number in the lower, right-hand corner. The next page should contain a table of contents that lists the page where each primary section can be found. If these primary sections consist of many pages and exhibits, tabs should separate the pages. The text of your business plan should not contain any errors. Proofread the text several times to be sure all of your content is correct. Each page should be numbered and printed on white stock paper. If you have a logo or other trademark, it should be printed on the cover of your presentation binder. (Local office supply stores such as *Office Depot*, *OfficeMax*, and *Staples* sell the supplies to make a business presentation binder.)

If you are making a formal business presentation, have one copy of the completed presentation binder for each person attending and one for yourself. (It is usually a good idea to bring extra copies of the presentation binder so that the attendees can bring one back to their boss.) You may also want to use exhibits such as samples of your product, overhead projector slides, or a computer power point presentation.

Using PowerPoint. PowerPoint presentations are done using specific computer software. The software will provide instructions as to how to set up the presentation. However, if you are not comfortable with computer equipment or software, do not attempt this type of presentation. Being in front of an audience is stressful enough without having to worry about computer glitches. (If you do decide to use a PowerPoint presentation, make a contingency plan in case the computer does not work.)

QUICK Tip

Pay Attention to EVERYONE: If your product is edible, make sure to bring enough to feed three or four times the number of people who are attending the presentation. Why? So that the attendees assistants and secretaries can enjoy your product. In business, it is often the associates' good words about a product that will influence the boss.

Presenting Your Plan. During the verbal presentation, go through the presentation binder in the order it is printed. Do not jump around from page to page. Assume that your audience can read—do not read it word-for-word. Touch on the highlights of each section; explain graphs and exhibits; and, offer your opinion on how profitable your business can be.

When you have gone through the entire binder, ask for questions. If you get a question that you cannot answer right away ask for the person's name and number so that you can get back to him or her with an answer. (Provide the answer within twenty-four hours.) Once all the questions have been answered, thank everyone for their presence and offer to answer any additional questions they may have, privately.

Informal Presentations

You may be asked to present your business plan in an informal setting such as for a networking organization, for a business society, or even as part of a career day for a school. Again, the first step is to know your audience. The next step is to make sure that your business plan presentation is understandable and does not talk down to your audience.

For a business society or networking organization, the layout of your presentation document is roughly the same as with the formal document, only it is usually not in a binder. For the more informal presentations, usually the title page also contains the name of the organization to whom you are presenting and the date of the presentation.

As with the formal presentation, you will verbally go through the written material hitting the highlights and asking for questions. For career day presentations, you may also want to share with the audience why you decided to become part of the specific industry, how much education the job requires, and what they can do to get more information.

Putting Your Business Plan to Work

A complete plan has three basic uses for your new business: communication, management, and planning. As a *communication device*, your plan will help you lay out the activities you need to accomplish; state your financial goals with clarity; and, reveal how much *working capital* (money to meet your expenses) you need. Your plan can also be used to communicate to potential lenders your mission and how you plan to use their money in your home-based business.

While you are building your plan, you will need to take a realistic look at every phase of your business. The process you go through to build your plan lets you take an impartial, serious, and unflustered look at what you are thinking about doing. It will enable you to work out all the problems you see and decide on potential options before actually launching your home-based business. Putting solutions to problems into your plan will give you a communication tool to use as evidence that you are ready for whatever the future holds.

QUICK Tip

Communicate Your Goals: If you get to the point where you want to have partners or employees, you may want to use a business plan to communicate why they should join your business. If you want to collaborate with others, you can use it to communicate how they can fit into your business' goals and how they can benefit from the success of your operation.

To succeed in carrying out your management responsibilities, use your plan to monitor and evaluate your progress. Track your activities, income, and expenses. Compare them to what you have in your plan. By using your business plan to establish timelines and targets, you can measure your progress and compare your projections to your actual accomplishments.

Modify Your Business Plan: Use your plan as a living document that you can modify as you learn more about your business operations and gain experience functioning as a home-based business operator.

Use your business plan as a tool to guide you through the various phases of your business. It will allow you to work out a timeframe for when you will need funding. You will be able to use it to keep track of whether you are meeting your projected cash flow rate. You can use it to determine if you need to adjust your activities by adding a new product or service, working more hours, hiring help, or adjusting your spending.

Use your plan to give you a feel for timing—what you need to do by when. Think of your business plan as a road map of how to get from one small location called a dream to success.

BUSINESS PLAN

Summary

K&K Day Care Center will be formed in May 2007 in Oak Brook, Illinois. K&K Day Care Center is a corporation registered in the state of Illinois. Currently, the owners have accumulated $15,000 of start-up capital. It will be operated out of a residence at 244 South Orange Blossom Lane, owned by Katherine Phillips and her husband Daniel. The residence is a 5,000 square foot home. The Day Care Center will be located in the east portion of the first floor, in three rooms that are segregated from the rest of the house. This area has a large private bathroom and a separate entrance.

K&K is owned and operated by Katherine Phillips, a registered nurse with an advanced degree in pediatrics, and Karen O'Neill, a certified teacher with experience in teaching pre-school, first, and second grade. In addition to this team, K&K will have a full-time office administrator. Additional personnel, with teaching and/or nursing experience, will be hired as needed. The goal is one day care employee for every three to four children.

This business promises to be very lucrative for the following reasons.

1. Oak Brook is in the center of Illinois' "High Tech Corridor." It has more than 400 computer-related firms. These firms hire both men and women; many having young children. Our target market is these workers.

2. This city attracts workers from all around the northern Illinois area. For many of the workers their only day care option is near their home. This business would give them another option that is close to work and easy to access during lunch hours. K&K will encourage parents to spend lunchtime with their children.

3. K&K Day Care Center will be different from other day cares because it will also care for children who are ill. For these children we will require that the child be under a doctor's care; that the doctor certify that the illness is not contagious; and, provide us with other information. Because of the layout of this house, children who are ill will be cared for in a separate room.

We believe that we will bring a unique and needed service to this area—a reliable, close day care center that is there to help parents when they need it most. In two years, we anticipate that K&K will have the maximum number of children that we can care for. Based on that, we will need to expand our space in the third year.

Company Analysis

K&K Day Care Center will be a special place for parents, who work in Oak Brook, to take their children during the workday. It will be staffed by professionals who have experience in teaching or nursing. Each child will get one-on-one attention from the staff members. At K&K we will not just watch a child, we will help the child learn through organized classes presented by our teachers. If the child has a non-contagious illness, our nurses will care for that child so that the parents can go on to work.

The business is a corporation with Katherine Phillips as president and Karen O'Neill as senior vice president. James O'Neill, a Certified Public Accountant, will handle the company books and financial reports. Ms. Sylvia Phillips Newton, Esq., a licensed Illinois attorney, will be the legal advisor and legal agent for the corporation. We will operate it as a service company with all profits going back into the company for the first five years.

We intend to market through newspaper ads in the Oak Brook Times. It is sent to every home and company in the Oak Brook area. We have already contacted this newspaper and they plan to do a full-page story on K&K as soon as we open our doors. We are also going to send a mailing to each company's Human Resource Department introducing ourselves and providing them with cards, brochures, and flyers to pass out to their employees.

Service

Our service is to care for children for those who work in the city of Oak Brook. We are different from other day care centers because: 1) we provide licensed teachers who will plan educational classes for the children; 2) we provide nurses who care for ill children; and, 3) we are close to the parent's workplace, which will add quality parenting time during lunch.

We have no competitors in this city. K&K will be in competition with the parents' current day care providers, who usually do not care for ill children. Our staff and their experience in both teaching and nursing will set us apart from any other day care center.

Industry Analysis

The day care center industry in Northern Illinois is mostly individual moms who take in children while caring for their own. As for day care corporations, there is the ABC Kiddie Care with several locations in office buildings in downtown Chicago. ABC, similar to K&K, is close to where the parents work, and encourages parent/child lunches. Only four of the eleven ABC facilities are equipped to handle ill children with nurses on staff. According to "Chicago Financial" these four locations are the top revenue makers of the ABC Kiddie Care Corporation.

Market Analysis and Strategy

Our potential customer base is the technical and management workers who have jobs in the computer industry that dominates the city of Oak Brook and the surrounding area. These potential customers are highly educated, with many having Masters degrees in Computer Science or Engineering. They have a high income, usually over $90,000 per year. These people live outside the structured cities in some of the surrounding suburbs that offer multi-acre estates.

Our potential customers on average spend in excess of $25,000 per year on their young children (infant to six years old), mostly in the area of educational toys. An example is the expensive "Teaching Lizard" computer system for children six months to seven years old. This computer system cannot be produced in sufficient quantities for the demand of our potential customers.

Our market analysis shows that these people put their children's needs first. As customers, the most preferred way to approach this group is through their work location and by word-of-mouth. We will be contacting each company's Human Resource department in order to get the word of our service out to their employees. We are designing a brochure and flyer for this purpose. Our other primary marketing will be through the local Oak Brook newspaper, that is delivered to each company in the city. We believe that once the word of our service gets out, we will pick up many customers as our service is necessary and unique.

Management/Ownership

Currently the management of K&K Day Care Center will reside with the owners. Katherine Phillips, president, and Karen O'Neill, senior vice president, are both the owners and the primary managers of K&K. K&K plans to hire an office administrator who will be responsible for answering phones, filing, and other clerical functions. Future members of our staff will be required to have experience and current state licenses in either teaching or nursing.

Other members of management team includes James O'Neill, a Certified Public Accountant, and Ms. Sylvia Phillips Newton, Esq.

Attached are résumés and copies of current licenses from:
Katherine Phillips
Karen O'Neill
James O'Neill
Sylvia Phillips Newton, Esq.

Expansion Goals

K&K Day Care Center's success will be measured by the number of children we have scheduled to use the service and the number that are on the waiting list. We hope to always have a waiting list of at least five parents who want to get their children into the day care center. Knowing that we have five potential customers, will allow us to weather the normal changes in the number of children that most day care facilities deal with on an annual basis.

In three years, we want to be in a position of needing a larger facility so that we can accommodate the number of people on our waiting list. At that time, we also want to be considered as a place for nursing students to do a term of on-the-job training in their profession.

In five years, we want to be able to franchise our facility to other locations where there is a large concentrations of office workers.

Financial Analysis

Currently K&K has $15,000 of operating capital. That will go for baby and small child furniture. We will also need current educational material for our children. As of today we do not have the capital to hire a full time professional office administrator, which would be approximately $15.00 hour. However, Cindy Phillips, a high school junior has agreed to work in the clerical end of the business to help us out.

Attached are copies of:
Items which are needed to open our doors and their cost;
Our budget for the first year, prepared by our CPA; and,
Our price schedule per child for using the day care facility.

Schedule of Implementation

The date that K&K Day Care Center opens depends upon our getting a business loan. We anticipate that we will receive the loan in March and open our doors in May. We selected May as many children will be out of school and parents will be struggling with finding a proper day care facility.

Our first step, once the loan is received, is to purchase all the items on the attached list, have the printer print our brochures and flyers, and arrange for the local newspaper to do a story on our company.

While we are waiting for this loan, we are calling each company and obtaining a contact in the Human Resource Department so that we can send that person our information. In just doing this calling, we have generated quite a bit of interest in our service, already. We are also designing our brochure and writing our corporate policy book. That way we will be ready to start once the loan comes through.

Chapter

Make a Marketing Plan

Knowing who will buy your product and if others are selling the same item is basic to starting a home business. Once you determine who your customers are, you will need to set a price.

Determine the Marketability

To determine the marketability of your choice of product or service, you need to learn about your potential customers. There are four basic questions to help you determine the marketability of your mission.

1. What need does my service or product satisfy?
2. Who needs and can afford what I am offering?
3. Who has the authority to buy what I want to sell?
4. How accessible will my product or service be to my target market?

CASE STUDY: Specialty Bridal Veils

Mary Ann's Bridal Veils is a home-based business that makes one of a kind, specialty bridal veils and headpieces. These headpieces can be made to match any style of wedding dress and can be encrusted with antique lace, pearls, or precious gems. Mary Ann meets with the bride-to-be when she is selecting her wedding dress. Each headpiece is one of a kind. It is made especially for this one person and takes many hours to produce.

1. What need does my service or product satisfy?

Every bride needs a special veil and headpiece for her wedding. We provide a one-of-a-kind veil and headpiece that is designed just for that one exceptional bride. Our veils and headpieces are designed to match the wedding dress, to look perfect with the bride's features, and to become a treasured memento that can be passed down for generations. We can incorporate antique lace from France, material from the mother's and grandmother's wedding garb, material that matches the bride's wedding gown, material that matches the wedding party, ribbons, pearls, precious gems, and even diamonds for a one-of-a-kind exquisite headpiece. After the wedding, we will clean and store the headpiece.

2. Who needs and can afford what I am offering?

Women who are planning to get married are our customers. Because many women are getting married later in life this is the product for them. This product allows them to get a headpiece that is appropriate for the shape of their face and their lifestyle. It also allows the bride to honor her relatives by including parts of their wedding attire in the headpiece.

Because this would be an original (not ever to be duplicated) type of product, it would minimally cost twice as much as the usual wedding veil in the current marketplace. By adding pearls and gems, the price could be quite high. This product will appeal to those women who are older and may be paying for their own wedding.

3. Who has the authority to buy what I want to sell?
The decision-maker here is likely the bride-to-be or it could be the parents or relatives who are paying for the wedding.

4. How accessible will my product/service be to my target market?
Special bridal veils and headpieces will be shown at local bridal fashion shows. We will also take out a full page add in the national bridal magazines plus the local bridal magazines. Once a year, we will advertise in the pullout "Weddings" section in the newspaper. We will send brochures to the top bridal salons in the U.S. and will offer them a profitable vendor agreement.

QUICK Tip

Identify Your Customers' Characteristics: If your mission encompasses sales to a broader market, study the demographics of the area that interests you. Learn about the characteristics of a group of people by looking at the demographics of age, income level, education, and other traits of your potential target market from the U.S. Census Bureau at **www.census.gov**.

Once you do your market research, you will begin to get a picture of the marketplace for your dream. Knowing what you know now, do you like that picture enough to want to go ahead with the business idea or do you want to research another one?

Do Not Be Discouraged: If the first few ideas are not marketable, keep going back to your list. Research the ones that you ranked with high interest. Do not give up.

Learn About the Competition

Your competition is a major factor in your business decisions. A competitor that constantly undercuts you by lowering their price can ruin your business. You need to find out as much as you can about your competition. (Review Figure 8.1 to locate resources for obtaining competitive information.) Try to get the following information:

- the types of customers it attracts;
- the business' product or service, including the quality and price;
- its location;
- the vendors it uses; and (if important),
- the hours it is open to the public.

If you plan to have a seasonal business, determine how your competitors handle the cycles. If employees are in your plans, you will want to know:

- your competitor's salary for employees;
- the benefits provided by the competitor;
- the work hours;
- the skills required; and,
- your competitor's work place conditions.

Figure 8.1: SOURCES FOR COMPETITIVE INFORMATION

There are many sources of information about your competitors. The ones most frequently used by soon-to-be business owners on tight budgets include:

- Business directories
- Trade and Professional Associations
- Libraries
- Census Data
- Local Small Business Administration (SBA) district offices
- The competitors' brochures, pamphlets, and advertisements
- The competitors' websites, links to other sources
- The competitors' customers
- Your network

You need as much information as you can assemble about your potential competition on all levels. Never assume facts, or guess. Get hard, solid facts.

CASE STUDY: Analysis of the Competition

A small, start-up business in Georgia designed a curriculum product to help children learn to read. The founder did a quick analysis of the competition. It was a phone survey of school district administrators. This revealed that the only competitor had been in place for many years and teachers liked it. The start-up company's founder was not discouraged. He decided to market the unique features of the curriculum and to launch a public relations program to educate the community about how technology could help their children learn to read.

Alert!

Be Aware of Economic Conditions: A change in the economy can have a direct impact on you and on your competition. If your markets dry up, thin out, or just disappear, you will find it extremely difficult to continue with your current business model.

Spot Trends

Trends is another term for what the customer wants and purchases. How do you know what the customer wants? Listen to what customers say. If you can visit your competition, keep your ears open to customer comments. If you hear customers ask for products in large sizes or with a particular detail, you have spotted a trend. Go to places where your potential customers are and observe. Make friends. Ask questions. The list of information in Figure 8.2 will give you a good start in developing a survey to record your findings.

Figure 8.2: PLAN A SURVEY

Here's a way to do three things at once—find customers, identify their wants, and sell.

- Take a few samples and show them to friends, strangers, and business people in the network you are developing.

- Ask each person if they would buy your product.

- Ask them a varied set of questions about your proposed service or product.

Answers to these questions will help find customers, identify their needs, and determine their interest in purchasing your product or service.

Another way to spot a trend is to know whom your customers admire. For example, if you are marketing to the preteen shopper, watch TV programs that are aimed at this market. You may be able to spot the next hot item being worn, read, or listened to by a pop star, or advertised on the program.

Subscribe to Industry Publications and Join Industry Associations

Above all, know your industry. You cannot spot a trend unless you have an understanding of what in going on in your industry. As a business owner you must keep up with the news in your industry. You do this by subscribing to trade publications, belonging to associations in your industry, and from information gotten free from the Internet. *FORTUNE* magazine is a great source for small businesses. It produces a *Fortune Small Business E-Newsletter* that is full of ideas and information for small and home businesses. Visit the website at **www.fsb.com** or **www.fortune.com**.

Make Use of the Internet

Netscape, at **www.netscape.com**, also has a great deal of business information. It ranges from business ideas to current trends to a list of other small businesses that you may want to network with. The *Netscape Yellow Pages* is also another way to get free marketing. You can add your business name, address, and some information to their listing of businesses. (Currently, this service is offered with cost.)

Use Your Company Website

As simple as it sounds, you can determine what customers want by just asking them. If you have a website for customers to visit and order from, use this as a forum to find out what customers are looking for. Do you know how many potential customers visit your site, but don't buy? Do you know how many potential customers just only print a copy of your prices from your website? (Your website designer may be able to supply this type of information by merely installing simple counters in the site coding.) Potential customers who merely look at your site and go away are lost sales. Include a spot on your website where these potential customers can let you know what they are looking for.

QUICK Tip

Ask for Customers' Suggestions: Include the following kinds of questions on your website.

- *Did you find what you are looking for?*
- *What other products would you be interested in?*
- *How can we personally assist you?*

Think Outside the Box

One common trick in marketing is taking something that is relatively popular and finding a new use for it or putting a new spin on it. This can give you the loyal market of the original product plus the new-use market.

One example is the non-stick cooking spray. Originally marketed just for indoor cooking, the makers now advertise its uses for outdoor grills, and even to remove sticky labels.

This common business phrase is known as *thinking out of the box*. This is what the home-business owner needs to do when considering his or her product or service. Do not accept the traditional uses and the traditional market for your product. Look at current needs of various types of people. Determine how you might be able to create a need for your product. (Remember, even Eskimos need ice makers.)

Write a Marketing Plan

Writing a marketing plan revolves around three steps. Step one—gather and organize data by topic. Step two—analyze your findings. Step three—draft a marketing plan that uses the data you collected and the analysis it provided.

Gather and Organize Data

There are three main objectives in gathering data for your marketing plan: create a detailed overview (the big picture); identify your potential customers; and, decide upon your budget and methods to implement your plan.

1. Construct the Big Picture for Your Home-Based Business

- Describe your product or service in detail. Be specific. If you will have both a service and a product, describe them. For example, if you intend to paint and sell your artwork, you could also sell your services as a framer for which you could charge extra. Or, you could factor framing into the cost of the retail price and sell your picture and its frame as a package. Explain what people tell you about your proposed service or product. Show how you plan to turn negative reactions into opportunities.

- Identify your geographic marketing area—local, statewide, regional, national, or international. (Remember, that with the Internet available as a marketing tool, there are no geographic limitations for products.)

- Examine your competitive research. Lay out the information—price, quality, availability, reputation, expertise, target market—about businesses that are selling the same or similar product or service. Compare what your competitors charge to what you want to charge and decide whether your price will be the same or different. Determine what makes your product or service special or unique.

- Many special events occur during the year that may provide an opportunity for you to do your research. Attend events such as festivals, fairs, arts and craft shows, conferences, parades, and sports, community, and charitable events.

2. Identify Your Customers

- Once you decide to make a specific product or sell a particular service, you have a potential customer in mind. For example—if you make gourmet chocolates your customers are those who eat chocolate. If you offer a child-oriented service, your customers are people with children.

- Depending on your business or service, you may want to use more corporate-oriented methods of determining your market. Describe in detail the characteristics of the people who will want your product or service. List the demographics of your prospective customers: their age, gender, income, neighborhood, country, and language.

- Once you identify the characteristics of your target market, you need to get specific information about it. You will need this information to evaluate prospects and decide if you can tailor your sales approach to them.

Get Professional Advice: Librarians can help you choose possible databases. They can also guide you to the locations of those databases.

- List the qualities (selection, convenience, service, reliability, availability, affordability) your customers value and those your customers like least about your product or service. Describe what you can do to adjust your proposed product or service so you can serve your customers better.
- Do a *market survey*. The easiest and least expensive way to do a market survey is to ask friends and strangers if they would buy your product or service.

CASE STUDY: Mrs. Fields

The founder of Mrs. Fields Cookies started by giving away samples in order to see if people would pay for her cookies. People were not buying on the first day, so she created a market by giving away her cookies. She did not commission an expensive market survey, but relied on her own hard work.

- Describe the ways your potential customers are likely to learn about your product or service—print or media advertising, direct mail, phone book, word-of-mouth, referrals, Internet, trade shows, conferences of professionals, telemarketing, etc.

3. Prepare Your Marketing Budget

- Calculate the amount of money you can afford to put into your marketing budget. Use your sales estimates and compare them to what advertising and promotion costs could be. Calculate how much you plan to spend on marketing to reach each paying customer. In the first year, do not be surprised if you can find little money to put into your marketing budget. Take advantage of the free marketing by word-of-mouth, referrals, and networking.

QUICK Tip

Identify Your Marketing Objectives: The three objectives you should include your plan are: how will you communicate your message; what steps will you take to create an awareness of your product or service; and, what will you do to motivate people to buy what you are selling.

4. Identify Marketing Methods

- *Advertising* is a great way to get the word out about your product or service. In many cases, your customers will not know about your business' offerings unless you advertise. Many people with new businesses start out by putting a great deal of money into advertising. This creates huge bills up front. If you sign a contract for long-term advertising, you will be putting money out for a considerable length of time.
- *Mailing lists* are a good way to identify sales leads. You can usually rent a list from a list broker. These brokers are often listed in the Yellow Pages. You can discuss your product or service and the types of buyers you are looking for with them.
- Evaluate *direct mail promotion* as a tool. While it can be expensive, a direct mail promotion that can have a minimal cost is the company newsletter.

CASE STUDY: Newsletters

St. Charles Nursery and Landscaping, Inc. sends a quarterly newsletter to customers whose addresses they have because the people either signed a guest book or asked to be put on a mailing list. Their newsletter has helpful seasonal hints about plants, gardening, and landscaping. It always contains a discount coupon for newsletter subscribers.

- Consider *paid advertising* on radio, in print, on television, the Internet, in the Yellow Pages, and on billboards. If you want your service or product to be used by the audience who listens to your local public broadcasting station, you might want to consider a donation that is acknowledged on air. Ads in local media, including newspapers, can be pricey. Sometimes, local news media like to profile new businesses in articles.

Analyze Data

The reason to gather and organize data is to use it to make your business successful. Following are some ways to use the data you have gathered.

1. Use the Big Picture. Going through the exercise of constructing the big picture or an overview of your business and your product, is more than just mental gymnastics. That overview can help to determine a catch phrase when describing your business. This is useful in any networking situation, for example "Hi I'm Nancy, I make the best fudge brownies in the tri-state area." (These quick overviews can also become the material that you use in press releases. For example: "Nancy Jones, owner of the cookie shop that makes the best fudge brownies in the tri-state area, announces a new location on Main Street.")

Along with the description of your product, you have identified your initial market. That information can be used to select where you want to advertise. Geographic information can also become a goal for your business. You may decide that once you achieve a certain dollar amount in your initial geographic area, then you are ready to market your product in a larger area.

Analyzing the competition is a great use of the data you have gathered. By looking at the competition you can get an idea of what is currently selling and the price that the marketplace is willing to pay for these goods. You want to make your product or service somehow different from the competition. This can be done by adding to the product or changing the price. As long as your business has competition, you should continually look at what they are selling and how you can make your product better.

2. Identify your customers. Customer data can also be used as a direction to grow your company. This can be done by marketing to different customers than those who normally purchase your goods, by making changes to your product or by adding more products to your line.

An example would be a can opener that has been marketed to strictly baby boomers. Unfortunately now the baby boomers are getting older and many have problems with arthritis. In order to maintain baby boomers as the primary customers the maker of the can opener may decide to update the product with an easy to grip handle.

Another example of this in a professional home-based business is the attorney who concentrates on wills and estate planning for the elderly. That attorney may decide to expand the business by advertising a package to younger people that includes planning for future health care options along with protection of assets.

3. Prepare a marketing budget and identify the various marketing methods you will use. The information is gathered by looking at how each type of advertising works in your profession. Once you have identified the marketing methods, the cost of each, and how those marketing methods work in your industry, you can determine which ones you want to use. (As you will discover, not all marketing methods produce the same result for every business.)

One last word about gathering and using data. Once you have gone through the effort to get the information and used it in your planning, save it and keep it updated. After your business is up and running, you may notice a change in customers. Make a note of that in the original customer data. You should also make notes of changes in competition. As you try different approaches to marketing your business, keep track of what worked and what did not. Keeping this information current will be of great assistance as you market your business in the future. (You may find that a very expensive method of marketing that you passed up at the opening of your business is now affordable because of the changing marketplace.)

Advertise to Your Customers: When it comes to paying for ads, make sure the ads will reach customers who would use your product or service. See if you can try out a type of advertising for a month or two and keep records of how many customers each ad brought in. Begin small.

Home-Based Business Marketing Plan

This is the marketing plan of _____

I. MARKET ANALYSIS

A. Target Market - Who are the customers?

1. We will be selling primarily to (check all that apply):

Total % of Business

☐ a. Private sector _____%

☐ b. Wholesalers _____%

☐ c. Retailers _____%

☐ d. Government _____%

☐ e. Other _____%

2. We will be targeting customers by:

☐ a. Product line/services. We will target specific lines _____

_____

☐ b. Geographic area? Which areas? _____

_____

☐ c. Sales? We will target sales of _____

_____

☐ d. Industry? Our target industry is _____

_____

☐ e. Other? _____

_____

3. How much will our selected market spend on our type of product or service this coming year? $_____

B. Competition

1. Who are our competitors?

Name _____

Address _____

Years in business _____

Market share _____

2. The following are some important legal factors that will affect our market:

_____

_____

_____

3. The following are some important government factors:

_____

_____

_____

4. The following are other environmental factors that will affect our market, but over which we have no control:

_____

_____

_____

II. PRODUCT OR SERVICE ANALYSIS

A. Description

1. Describe here what the product/service is and what it does:

_____

_____

_____

B. Comparison

1. Describe the advantages your product/service have over those of the competition (consider such things as unique features, patents, expertise, special training, etc.):

_____

_____

_____

2. What disadvantages does it have?

_____

_____

_____

_____

C. Some Considerations

1. Where will you get your materials and supplies?

_____

_____

2. List other considerations:

_____

_____

_____

_____

III. MARKETING STRATEGIES - MARKET MIX

A. Image

1. First, what kind of image do we want to have (such as cheap, but good, exclusiveness, customer-oriented, highest quality, convenience, or speed)?

_____

_____

_____

_____

B. Features

1. List the features we will emphasize:

a. _____

b. _____

c. _____

d. _____

C. Pricing

1. We will be using the following pricing strategy:
   a. Markup on cost _____ What % markup? _____
   b. Suggested price _____
   c. Competitive _____
   d. Below competition _____
   e. Premium price _____
   f. Other _____

2. Are our prices in line with our image?
   YES _____ NO _____

3. Do our prices cover costs and leave a margin of profit?
   YES _____ NO _____

D. Customer Services

1. List the customer services we provide:
   a. _____
   b. _____
   c. _____
   d. _____

2. These are our sales/credit terms:
   a. _____
   b. _____
   c. _____
   d. _____

3. The competition offers the following services:
   a. _____
   b. _____
   c. _____
   d. _____

E. Advertising/Promotion

1. These are the things we wish to say about the business:

_____

_____

_____

_____

_____

2. We will use the following advertising/promotion sources:

☐ Television _____

☐ Radio _____

☐ Direct mail _____

☐ Personal contacts _____

☐ Trade associations _____

☐ Newspaper _____

☐ Magazines _____

☐ Yellow Pages _____

☐ Billboard _____

☐ Other _____

3. The following are reasons why the media we have chosen is considered to be the most effective:

_____

_____

_____

_____

_____

Truth in Advertising

The Federal Trade Commission has publications that you can get to study truth in advertising in general and for some individual industries. For example, mail order and telephone sales are two of those industries that are popular for home-based businesses to use. Your ads must be truthful, fair, and nondeceptive. You need to have and keep evidence of your advertised claims.

QUICK Tip

Federal Advertising Laws: To get information about federal advertising laws, contact the Federal Trade Commission at **www.ftc.gov**. In addition, two good sources of free information about your state's requirement are its consumer protection department and the attorney general's office.

Advertising Concerns

To avoid deceptive advertising, there are two essential rules. First, do not use a statement or omit information that is likely to mislead consumers who are acting reasonably under general circumstances. Second, do not use a deceptive statement that is important to a consumer's decision to buy or use your service or product.

Labeling can be an advertising issue. On your product's label, be accurate about the type and quantity of ingredients you use. For food labeling information, contact the Food Marketing Institute at 202-452-8444 or online at **www.fmi.org**. Contact your local weights and measures officials for information about inspection procedures that you might need to have done before you can advertise food.

If there are harmful substances in your product, they must be disclosed on the label. Size and style of warning print could be an issue. Your state and the federal Environmental Protection Agency will have information about how to label your product if it has ingredients harmful to humans.

Some professions limit what their members can advertise. For example, dentists are constricted on what they claim about TMJ treatment expertise. There could be consequences with professional licensing or membership in professional associations.

If you advertise a product that claims to have a manufacturer's rebate, be sure the manufacturer is honoring that rebate and is doing it in a reasonable period of time. The Federal Trade Commission can sanction you for a manufacturer's failure to pay the rebate.

Customers are FREE Advertising: Referrals and return customers can be the most cost effective advertising and promotion campaign that you will ever have.

Implementing Your Marketing Plan

Prioritize the marketing tools you have identified. Review your budget, and then choose a focus or theme for your campaign. Then launch your advertising and promotional activities. Once you choose a focus, then you need to plan your activities. Review the steps in Figure 8.3 in order to effectively implement your marketing plan.

Figure 8.3: STEPS TO IMPLEMENT YOUR MARKETING PLAN

1. Determine who your customers are. (Who would buy your product or service? Who are you trying to sell to?)

2. Identify the type of advertising and promotional activities to which your specific customers would respond. (Most business people read business magazines, business sections of the newspaper, and may watch TV shows that deal with business issues. A slick brochure given out to commuters at the train station may influence these business people.)

3. Narrow the list of promotional activities you selected in #2, by obtaining basic information such as:

   - cost;

   - what is required to use their advertising;

   - how long an ad runs; and,

   - how you can create the material.

4. Create your ad or promotional brochure and partner with the advertising opportunities you have selected.

5. MOST IMPORTANT. Ask every customer how he or she heard about you. Keep track of which marketing tool worked the best.

Networking

Networking is the business term used to describe what many people do naturally—develop or create contacts. When you communicate with them for advice, information, or support, you are networking. When you share information about yourself and your business, you are networking.

QUICK Tip

Networking is Your Lifeline: Small business owners who survive and thrive in even the most economically and emotionally challenging times are those who learn how to make networking a vital tool. This is true for them during their start-up phase, as well as later on.

Networking Methods

There is no end to the number of ways you can network. In this day and age, contacts can even be made through computers. Whatever method you use, stay focused on gathering the information you have set out to acquire. Some suggestions on the specific things you can do include the following.

- Join a professional or trade association (many offer lower dues to new members) and go to their local and national conferences.
- Attend network meetings where the only charge is for the food.
- Join a special interest group and attend the meetings and events.
- Join community groups.
- Join business groups like the American Business Women's Association, Rotary Club, or your local Chamber of Commerce.
- Join a mailing list server such as Listserv or Majordomo.

If your potential list of network contacts seems endless, that is great! Perhaps you have never thought of the people you know as being part of various networks, but they are. Many networks overlap. A good reputation can make your business successful. A bad reputation can ruin you.

It is important that you use the networking methods that are most comfortable for you. If you try to network in ways that make you uncomfortable, you will avoid making the contacts at all.

First Impressions

Although you may think it sounds trivial, eye contact and a firm handshake are key components of successful networking. Think about it. When someone holds out a limp hand, what is your reaction? How do you feel if people study their feet as they introduce themselves to you? True, if you have time to talk and get to know them better, you may find you have lots in common and enjoy their company immensely. Unfortunately, many excellent networking opportunities are very brief.

Make the most of those brief encounters. Smile as you look into the person's eyes. Use a firm handshake. As you greet them, repeat the person's name out loud. It will tell that person that you are interested in meeting them. You will also have a better chance of remembering their name.

Business Cards

If possible, get business cards. Several computer programs allow you to make your own. At this stage of your business, you really need only a bare bones business card with your personal name and phone number. When you network face-to-face the tradition is to exchange business cards. This is an important part of the contact for both people. It is simple for you to go home and enter the other person's name and record the information. You may find it helpful to take some action—follow up with a letter, handwritten note, or email. That follow-up will help fix the conversation in that person's memory and further cement the contact.

Make sure you use this early networking time to talk about your business and answer questions about who you are. This is a prime opportunity to tell people about your mission.

Set Your Pricing Policy

To calculate what you will charge for your product or service, determine the number of hours you will have to work to meet your expenses, to pay your taxes, and to make a profit. At the point where you are able to pay all of your expenses and tax liabilities is the amount at which you will break even. Any amount over what you set as your break even level is profit.

The price you set must reflect what it costs you to make, sell, and deliver your product. If you are in a service business, you will need to factor in all of your costs, including your time. Then you can decide upon a cost per unit, an hourly rate, a flat fee, a contract price, or other formula typically used by people in your line of business. Look to your budget to review what your costs are. Calculate the number of units of your product you will need to make or number of hours you will need to provide to reach your income goal and pay all of your bills.

If you are in a service business and will be charging hourly, you will need to determine your rate. See if it is possible to learn what others in your line of work are charging. Professional and trade conferences are often good places to collect this data as people who attend them might be forthcoming with this information. People who have purchased your type of service from your potential competitors may be willing to tell you what they paid.

Keep in mind, the rates you learn about may not be correct for your situation because your budgeted costs may be less or more than theirs. (Costs are often called *overhead*.)

Review your budget every month or so to stay current with your overhead expenses, like insurance, advertising, office supplies, your pay, phone, rent, supplies, equipment, advertising, postage, and travel for the business as a whole. You may want to adjust your pricing—downwards (to meet or beat the competition) or upwards (to be able to pay yourself, your taxes, and all other bills).

What the Market Will Pay

Regardless of what your pricing policy is, what others will pay for your good or service is the *bottom line*. There are many ways to determine what that price is. Start by finding out what others charge who do the same kind of work or sell the same types of items that you plan to sell.

Your Competition

Part of the research you have done was to look at what the competition is charging for the same item or service. If the amount they are charging is so low that you know you cannot meet this amount and still make money, consider adding something different to your item or service.

CASE STUDY: Candy Sales

In a metropolitan area a specific candy is selling for $20 a pound. Sandy has a recipe for a homemade version of the candy, but at a sale price of $20 a pound she is barely breaking even. Sandy needs to identify some way to separate her product from the rest of the market place. She may want to emphasize her product is homemade or from a family recipe. She may package it differently—say a smaller amount of candy in a fancy tin whereby she could charge $15 for a half pound.

Pricing Information Sources

Potential customers can be sources of information about pricing. Ask them about your pricing or what they will pay for what you plan to sell. Stay focused on their current needs and expectations. If you think that as a new business you need to attract customers by offering deals on prices, do it. Just be sure your cash flow projections are based on those figures. You can always raise prices when you think your customer base is ready.

QUICK Tip

Business Information Services: This is another time to check with your local SBA District Office Business Information Centers (BIC). They have reference material that can help you with pricing your product. Call 800-827-5722 for the BIC nearest you or go online at **http://sba.gov**.

Trade associations are another good resource for pricing information. Many trade associations have how-to manuals on pricing accuracy. For example, if you are in the food preparation business, contact the Food Marketing Institute at 202-452-8444 or online at **www.fmi.org**. If you sell a product at the consumer level, contact the National Retail Federation at 202-783-7971 or online at **www.nrf.com**. If you are selling food at the retail level, contact your local weights and measures officials for information about inspection procedures as well as pricing laws. For a copy of the price verification procedures contact the National Conference on Weights and Measures at **www.nist.gov/owm**.

Be aware that even after you have done all the research and have been in business for a while, you may discover that your pricing levels are wrong—too high or too low. Stay flexible. Change whenever you think it is appropriate. Be sure to make those changes in your marketing plan and in your business plan.

Discounts

Discounts are a time-honored business practice. Discounts are a way a home-based businesses can attract new business, reward large volume customers, encourage new customers to try your product for the first time, or meet your competition's practices.

Some industries have a tradition of giving discounts to certain types of customers or for particular products or services. Research what the discounting practices are in your industry. You then must decide if you want to meet that discount or add value to your service or product to keep your price at a premium.

Discounts and Your Budget: If you decide to give a discount, be sure that your budget reflects the amount of the discounted price. This is very important, especially if there will be a substantial effect upon your projected income.

Legal Issues for Pricing

There may be state and federal laws that control aspects of your pricing. Most of these laws approach pricing within the context of advertising and promotion. The goals are to protect the consumer and provide your business with guidelines on how to design your pricing and advertising so that they are fair and not deceptive.

Promoting a Sale

A typical way to encourage people to buy your product is to have a *sale*. A real sale is when you reduce the price of the products that you sell. If the former price is the actual, valid price you were selling it at to the public on a regular basis for a reasonable and substantial period of time, it provides a legitimate basis for the advertising of a price comparison. But, if the former price being advertised is not genuine, there is no bargain. For example, if you create a make believe, inflated price so that you can claim you are offering a product for a big reduction, the so-called bargain that you then advertise is false and not legal.

Commenting on Your Competitor's Price

If you advertise that you are selling a product at a price lower than your competitors, be sure that the price you advertise is what a consumer would consider a genuine bargain or saving. For example, if several of your competitors regularly sell variety F flower bulbs at $20.00 a dozen, it is honest for you to advertise: "Variety F flower bulbs—priced elsewhere $20.00; our price $16.99."

Keeping Prices Fair

The laws that govern pricing do not allow you to deceive or mislead people. Your prices must be real. You cannot advertise one price and then sell for a higher one. For example, if one of your products or services usually sells for $19.95, it is illegal to say that it usually sells for $29.95, but now you are willing to sell it for the bargain price of $19.95.

Alert!

Bait and Switch: Do not pull a bait and switch. You cannot advertise an item for one price and then try to sell a substitute item of lesser quality at the same or higher price.

Buy one get one free is a favorite inducement. In addition, it is legal. However, do not increase the price of an item or service, and then offer a second for free. Do not make the second one of lesser quality. This once "acceptable business practice" is now illegal.

Penalties for Deceptive Pricing Practices

There are some serious penalties for engaging in deceptive pricing practices. Your state and the federal government can levy fines against you. Both of them can order you to cease and desist your practice and fine you if you do not comply. Consumers can sue you for the damages they incur because of your practices. One of the worst penalties can be the resulting bad publicity for you and your business if you are fined or sued for this kind of practice.

Set a Fair Price: Use the price that is ethical in your line of business and in your community. If yours is a unique product or service in your community, do not set the price you want to charge to the level of gouging. Conversely, do not set it so low that you will unfairly short change yourself.

Tracking Your Prices

It is surprising how many small business owners do not know the exact price of each component that goes into their product. Attorneys don't know how long it takes to produce a type of document; cookie makers don't know the cost of the sugar; office cleaners don't know the cost of a big box of garbage bags. Anything that goes into producing your product or service should be broken down into the cost per item and/or length of time it takes to make it.

CASE STUDY: Pricing

It takes $20 worth of cooking supplies and two hours to make ten big cookies. You sell the cookies for $2 a piece. In this situation, your time is worth nothing and you have made nothing on the sale after deducting expenses. With this analysis, you can quickly determine that you have not priced your product in a fair manner.

If you do not know the costs and time put into your product you will never know when you are making money and when to raise your prices. Tracking increases in the cost of ingredients is also important, that tells you when you need to find a new supplier. Tracking the time spent on something tells you when your production is getting more efficient.

Chapter

Make a Financial Plan

Once you have your plan written, it is time to think about how to obtain the financing you need to start you home-based business. Budgeting that financial support will then follow.

▶ **Personal Savings**
▶ **Inheritance or a Gift**
▶ **Credit Cards**
▶ **Debit Cards and ATM Cards**
▶ **Equity in Your Home**
▶ **Loan from Family or Friends**
▶ **Buying on Time**
▶ **Renting or Leasing Equipment**
▶ **Line of Credit**
▶ **Retirement Funds**
▶ **Banks and Credit Unions**
▶ **The Small Business Administration**
▶ **Assistance for Veterans**
▶ **Budget**

Personal Savings

The first place to look for money is in your own pocket. Personal savings are those monies you have put aside for a rainy day into savings accounts, savings bonds, investment accounts, money market funds, and mutual funds. This source of capital is great. You have already saved this money. It is yours and you can do whatever you want with it.

If another person has the right to rely on those savings, talk with that person and negotiate the amount you can use for the new business. Be sure to discuss whether you will have to pay some or all of it back, perhaps with interest, and the date when you agree to start paying it back.

Using personal savings can give you independence from creditors and investors. It is probably the best way to go. It even could be worth your wait to implement your business plan until you build up your savings to the level you need to get going and will not diminish your rainy day fund any more than you have to.

Inheritance or a Gift

If a relative or friend has died and left you some money in a will, you might want to put your inheritance to work in your new venture. Some parents and grandparents who have the ability to leave an. inheritance may be pleased to give it to you during their lifetime, then they can enjoy seeing you build your dream with their help.

If you are lucky enough to have a relative or a friend give you money, there are a couple of precautions that you should take. There could be federal gift tax consequences to the person giving the money, if that individual person's gift to you exceeds $11,000. Check with your tax advisor and structure your plans accordingly. Have the person who gives you a gift, also give you a dated letter stating it is a gift. What you want is to make it clear that it is not a loan for you or your business. If the IRS or anyone else challenges the amount, you will have the letter to show that it was a gift, not a loan. Lastly, be sure to enter it into your books as a gift.

Credit Cards

Credit cards are a common resource that businesses use to purchase items. Using a credit card acts as a loan. If you pay off the balance each month, the loan is interest free. However, if you plan on using personal credit cards for business expenses, there are some serious downsides. The biggest challenge is to keep personal expenses separate from business ones—a critical step when it comes to taxes.

In addition, a credit card may offer you more protection than even cash. Many of the major credit card companies will help the consumer if an item bought with their credit card turns out to be defective or unusable. Some credit card companies will actually forgive a charge for a defective item and then go after the manufacturer with their large legal team.

Business Credit Card: Instead of using an existing personal credit card, it is a much better choice as a new business owner to get a credit card in the name of the business for business expenses only.

Beware of the New Bankruptcy Law: Using credit cards for start-up costs has become less attractive to new, home-based business owners as a result of the changes to the bankruptcy law passed in 2005. The law allows credit card companies to charge interest as high as 27%, if at any time you do not pay your balance in full and on time. In addition, you have to repay the bankruptcy debt before you can use money for anything beyond living expenses.

Credit Rating

If you do not pay your credit card bills on time, you can get a bad credit rating. In the future, you may want to get a loan for your business from a bank or other lending institution. However, you will need a good credit report to get a loan without much hassle. These errors could also end up on your credit report. You want to get them fixed immediately.

QUICK Tip

Credit Reporting Agencies: Contact (any and all) credit reporting agencies if you have questions about you credit report.

- Equifax at 888-685-1111 or www.equifax.com
- Experian at 888-397-3742 or www.experian.com
- TransUnion at 800-916-8800 or www.transunion.com

Debit Cards and ATM Cards

Debit cards allow a merchant to deduct the amount you charge directly from your checking account. These cards enable you to buy items when you need them without the hassle of paying with cash, personal check, or coping with maxed-out credit cards.

ATM cards let you withdraw money (24 hours a day/7 days a week) from an ATM machine. As with debit cards, make a record of each and every withdrawal, the date, amount, and business purpose at the time of the withdrawal. Be sure to note the withdrawal in your accounting books.

As opposed to credit cards, debit cards and ATM cards offer very little consumer protection. If someone takes a debit card or an ATM card they can, with the proper password, take all the funds out of your business' checking account.

A hybrid of these cards is offered by American Express. This card looks like a credit card, but functions like traveler's checks. The consumer purchases this travel card with a certain amount of cash. Then, instead of presenting travelers check for a purchase, the consumer uses this card. (Just like with traveler's checks, you can have the card replaced if stolen.)

Track Withdrawals: Keep track of each of your withdrawals. There may be tax consequences if you do not have a way to demonstrate on what the money was spent.

Equity in Your Home

You can get a loan for *equity* in your home or a *line of credit* for your equity. Equity is the difference between the amount of money left on your mortgage and what your home is now worth in the market. A line of credit is a loan that lets you access your equity. There are several positives to this choice.

You may be able to deduct the interest payments from your personal federal tax obligations for both of these. This feature is important as it reduces the effective cost of the loan to you. Even better, you can spend the loan proceeds on any purpose—including your business expenses. Your home is likely to be your largest, personal investment. It is also likely and to have grown in value since you bought it. You may have enough value in your home to fund some or all of your start-up costs.

However, the downside of these loans is that your home will be your collateral. In other words, you put your home ownership at risk. If you do not repay your loan, you could face loss of your home through foreclosure proceedings.

Loan from Family or Friends

Treat any friend or family member like you would any other lender. The upside to asking these people to invest in your business is that they know you and love you. The downside is that not all friends and family members are willing to treat a loan to you as a business proposition. And if things do not go well for you, the biggest downside is that you risk jeopardizing the relationship.

If, in your judgment, you can get a positive commitment to lend, set up that meeting right away for as soon as possible. Take two things with you to the meeting—your business plan and a blank *promissory note*. A promissory note is a legal agreement in which one person legally promises to repay a loan. It may include an amount of interest that also must be repaid. Promissory notes are as legal as writing a check. The person you give the note to can force you to repay the amount by taking you to court.

Promissory Note—Lump Payment

$_____   Date:_____, 20____

_____ hereby promises to pay to the order of _____ the sum of $_____, with interest thereon from the date of this note to the date of payment at the rate of _____ per annum.

   This note is due and payable in full on _____, 20___, if not paid sooner. The principal and interest shall be payable when due at _____ _____ or at a place of which the undersigned may be notified in writing by the holder of this note.

   This note is not assumable without the written consent of the lender. This note may be paid in whole or in part at any time prior without penalty. The borrower waives demand, presentment, protest, and notice. This note shall be fully payable upon demand of any holder in the event the undersigned shall default on the terms of this note or any agreement securing the payment of this note. In the event of default, the undersigned agrees to pay all costs of collection including reasonable attorneys fees.

   IN WITNESS WHEREOF, the undersigned has executed this note under seal as of the date stated above (if the undersigned is a corporation, this note has been executed under seal and by authority of its board of directors).

                              _____

                              _____

Used with permission from The Complete Book of Personal Legal Forms, M. Warda, 2005, Sphinx Publishing.

Decide before the meeting what you believe is a reasonable interest rate for you to pay the lender. From your business plan, you should be able to predict what period of time you will need before you have to pay the note and interest back. When you meet, be prepared to negotiate your request, including any periodic payment schedule.

Your no-nonsense, well-prepared, business-like approach to your family member or friend will give that person confidence in you and enhance your chances in getting the amount of a loan that you need.

Buying on Time

This is not a source of cash, but it is a way to enable you to purchase items you need. New businesses, just like more established ones, can buy from their suppliers and do it on credit. In fact, people in the construction business routinely buy on credit for each job they have a contract. A reliable and longtime customer is likely to get better terms than a new business, but a new business owner will often find a supplier's terms better than a credit card company's.

This method of financing purchases is sometimes called *buying on time*. The supplier will let you purchase supplies and not expect payment in full for thirty, sixty, or even ninety days. If a supplier charges you interest, it is likely to be less than a credit card company.

QUICK Tip

Negotiate Payment Terms: When the economy is bad, suppliers, like other merchants, are often ready to deal on payment terms. Negotiate the best payment terms you can.

Renting or Leasing Equipment

There are several upsides to renting or leasing. Just like the option to buying on credit, these two options allow you to spread payments over time. Renting or leasing equipment can be a valuable way to get what you need right away. You can free up large sums of money for other uses. If you do not have a lot of cash to spend or if using your credit to buy equipment is not possible, consider this option. You may not have storage space in your home for equipment that you need for a short period of time, so being able to rent for a day or two may be a great fit for your needs.

Line of Credit

A line of credit is a way to get a pre-approved loan on demand from your bank. When you establish your line of credit, your bank will tell you the exact amount you will have available. (Some banks refer to lines of credit in small amounts as *overdraft privileges*.)

A line of credit has a big upside. It allows you to write checks in amounts greater than what you have in your checking account. Because it is a pre-approved loan, you will have to pay interest on the funds you use. The interest starts on the day the check clears your bank and appears on your monthly statement.

Retirement Funds

While not the best option, it is true that your non-IRA retirement accounts may offer you some financial help. Some plans allow you to borrow against your retirement savings for business purposes. You might be able to borrow, with interest, from your pension, 401(k), or other plan the IRS has qualified. When you pay back interest, you will pay it back to yourself. However, many financial advisors believe that the payback to yourself will never equal the interest and growth your account would have made had you not borrowed from it.

Alert!

Withdrawing Retirement Funds: The tax benefits of contributing to a retirement plan may be destroyed if you cash in your account or borrow against it. You could incur stiff penalties that you have to pay to the IRS. In addition, if you do not repay what you withdraw, you put yourself at a distinct disadvantage when you need the funds in your later years.

Instead of borrowing against your retirement funds, you may be able to use them as collateral to secure a loan. Like any other collateral, you will put your retirement funds at risk of being seized by the lender if for any reason you can not repay the loan.

Banks and Credit Unions

Because your business will need to have a place for its checking account, a bank is a good place to start to look for a commercial loan. Some businesses make use of banking services much more than others do. You need to think through what you might use them for in your particular situation. Some banks will have a brochure listing the types of small business services that are available.

Credit unions are financial organizations that are membership groups composed of individuals who share a common bond such as an employer or a labor union. They provide their members with several types of bank services, such as checking and savings accounts and making loans. If you belong to a credit union or are eligible to belong to one because you share a common bond with its members, inquire about its menu of services, including loan practices. Figure 9.1 lists the general information a bank or credit union will need for an application for a loan.

Figure 9.1: LOAN APPLICATION

A typical, comprehensive loan application may ask you to provide the following information.

- Summary of your business

- Description of your industry, trade, or profession

- Product or service and your marketing plan

- Current financial picture, including all personal assets and liabilities and any prior bankruptcies

- Detailed budget for one year

- List of your property and an estimate of the current market value that you can offer to guarantee the loan

---

continued

- Management expertise and the ownership of your new business
- Business entity
- Current or potential intellectual property rights
- Detailed account of insurance
- Amount of any stock issued
- Names of attorneys and other consultants
- Amount of money you (and others) will invest in your business
- Amount of the loan you want
- What the loan will be used for

The Small Business Administration

The Small Business Administration (SBA) has several Small Business Development Centers (**www.sba.gov/sbde**) located in all fifty states, Washington, D.C., the Virgin Islands, and Puerto Rico. Through their programs, they provide management assistance to current and prospective small business owners. The SBA enables commercial banks to make loans to small businesses. It offers one-stop assistance to small businesses by providing a wide variety of information and guidance. To find the SBA office near you, look in your local phone book or call the SBA Answer Desk at 800-827-5722.

Assistance for Veterans

If you are a veteran, you can contact a Veterans Business Development Officer in the SBA District Office near you to help you prepare and plan your new business. The Veterans Business Outreach Program (VBOP) (**www.sba.gov/vets**) offers entrepreneurial enhancement services such as business training, counseling, and mentoring to eligible veterans who are thinking about starting a small business. To find out if you are eligible, call your Veterans Business Development Officer. Regardless of other veteran eligibility rules, *all* military veterans are eligible for consideration under SBA's guarantee loan program.

Budget

Once you have found ways to finance your business, you must decide how that money will be spent. This is the reason you need a *budget*. Having and following a budget will let you see how much money is needed, what the money is spent on, and when the bills are due. Having a budget for your business also shows those who are helping to finance your business that you will carefully spend their money.

To guide your budget preparation, ask the following questions.

- How much income will my business make?
- When will my cash flow start and at what rate will cash come in to my operation?
- When will I be able to cover my expenses?

To calculate the work you have to do to meet your income needs, ask yourself the following questions.

- How many units of my product or service do I need to sell?
- At what price do I need to sell each unit or service?
- How many units do I have to produce to meet my income goal?
- How many hours do I need to work?
- Will I be able to put at least six months of operating funds into reserves to use as a safety cushion for when cash flow does not meet expenses?
- What other categories of expenses will I have in my situation?

Budget preparation is made easier when you use software. So, one of the first steps in budget creation is to find a software program you like. You want one that is flexible, as easy to use as you need it to be, and can be tailored to your specific situation. To avoid hassles and wasting time, do not be tempted to buy a software program because you can get a good deal on it. Wait until you can afford the kind of software that has the features that you need in order to be successful.

QUICK Tip

Access to Computer Software: If you are unable to buy software in the timeframe that you need to get started, check with your local SBA District Office Business Information Center (BIC). You can often get access to state-of-the-art computer hardware and software at these facilities. Call 800-827-5722 for the BIC nearest you or go online at **http://sba.gov/region/states.html**.

To budget is to forecast the future. To make truthful forecasts, put accurate and realistic expense estimates into your budget. Make your very best guess at revenue projections for the year. You may need to estimate revenue on a quarterly or even more frequent basis. However, the quarterly estimate of revenue will match up with your requirement to file estimated taxes and calculate your income for your end-of-the-year tax filing.

Your budget will give you a feel for what your rate of cash flow will be. Cash flow is all the money that is used in your business. The flow is following the money from the moment that it comes in from customers through where it ultimately ends up. The cash can end up as funds to pay bills, salaries, or be put into a financial account as profit.

QUICK Tip

Positive Cash Flow: Think of cash flow as following each dollar bill as it goes from the customer's wallet into the business and then out to another business. In a negative cash flow situation, a business has too little money coming in to cover monthly bills and salaries. Businesses with negative cash flow do not make a profit.

Putting a budget together can be a challenge. However, it will give you a good idea of where you are and what you need to do to make your business succeed. Think of a budget as a living document. Revise it as often as you need to.

This budget worksheet was put together by a group of six people who started a painting business. They had no office. All were employees. One employee did the scheduling and billing from his home.

	Monthly Actual	Monthly Budget	Year-to-date Actual	Year-to-date Budget	Annual Budget
Revenue					
Residential					
Commercial					
Expenses					
Payroll					
FICA					
FUTA					
Benefits					
Insurance					
Truck Lease					
Answering Service					
Cell Phones					
Paint and Equipment					
Advertising					
Stationery					
Postage					
Accounting Assistance					
Legal Assistance					

CASE STUDY: Internet Expenses

Internet costs depend on the services your business will need and the amount of competition there is for your business. If you want a home page and email, get quotes from several Internet Service Providers (ISPs). How much do they charge per month for basic service? How many hours a month do you get for that fee? Will you need to use the net more than the hours they sell for a flat fee? If so, try to guess how much excess time you might use. If you discover you are way off in your projection after you have been operating for a few months, cut back or change the amount you allotted in your budget for this item.

Calculate Your Income

Revenues are an essential part of your budget. This is probably the most difficult projection you will have to make in your first few years. You have no accurate idea when you first start your business if it is going to earn what you hope. Think in terms of what you *can expect* the market will pay for the amount of goods or services you will be able to provide. (If you are setting up a franchise, the corporation will help with your business' calculations.)

What is revenue for your business will depend upon what your business does to earn it. Often, businesses sell a product or perform a service and are paid in cash. (For most tax purposes, checks and credit card payments are treated the same as cash.)

But what if you exchange your services or property with someone else? For tax purposes, the fair market value of what you receive is income to you. This type of income is called *barter*. If bartering is an option for you, think how that might work into your budget. Will it be a regular item or a one-time experience? Will it be what you judge as a small amount or a significant one? Will bartering be able to replace an item in your budget?

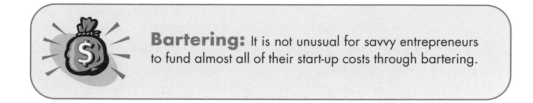

Bartering: It is not unusual for savvy entrepreneurs to fund almost all of their start-up costs through bartering.

A typical home-based, start-up business has the following categories of basic expenses.

- Salaries (including taxes (self-employment, FICA, income, corporate, unemployment) and retirement)
- Office expense (such as telephone and Internet)
- Furniture, office supplies, and equipment
- Inventory or manufacturing materials
- Consultant fees (such as legal fees, accounting fees, technical support)
- Insurance (such as health, property, liability, disability, and worker's compensation)
- Miscellaneous fees (such as licensing fees, professional association memberships, seminars, and publications)
- Transportation and travel expenses
- A six month cushion for operating and personal living reserves

Income-Based Budget

An income-based budget can be helpful for people who start businesses at home. The commitment at its heart is that you limit your expenses to the amount your income. This commitment can give you a sense of security.

To prepare your income-based budget, find answers to these questions:

- How much income will my business make?
- When will my cash flow start and at what rate will cash come in to my operations?
- When will I be able to cover my expenses?

To calculate your income projections, ask yourself the following questions.

- How many units of my product or service do I need to produce and sell to meet my financial goals?
- At what price do I need to sell each unit or service?
- How many hours do I need to work?
- How much will I need to spend on expenses (supplies/equipment/consultants/insurances/fees/travel/reserves)?

SECTION IV:

Put Your Plan into Action

Chapter 10

Legal Considerations

Specific legal steps must be taken in order to start a home-based business—selecting a business structure and registering your company with the state are only a few of them. These procedures not only fulfill necessary governmental regulations, but also will protect the home-based business owner.

▶ **State Registration**

▶ **Business Structure**

▶ **Employer Identification Number**

▶ **Licenses, Permits, and the Collection of Taxes**

▶ **Zoning Regulations**

State Registration

Registering your business with your state begins by deciding what type of business structure that your business will take and then filing the proper forms for your business with your state. Not all types of businesses are required to file with the state and not every state requires the same thing. Confused? Review the Secretary of State Internet site for your state. Some states provide a wealth of information for new businesses. (See the Appendix for a state-by-state list.)

Businesses register with the state for two important reasons—*taxes* and *liability*. Businesses may or may not be taxed differently than individuals—depending upon the type of business structure. For some it may save considerable tax payments to become a registered business.

Liability is your legal responsibility to those who are injured directly or indirectly from your products or services. Registering your business may protect you personally from another's injuries. While the business may be responsible, you are better situated to not lose your home or jeopardize your family's future if properly registered.

Business Structure

Your choice of business structure (entity) depends on your state requirements, who is legally involved in your business, and the level of personal liability you wish to assume. There are many types of business entities and not all are recognized in every state. The most common for the small, home-based business are the *sole proprietor* and the *limited liability company* (LLC). Other options include general partnership, limited liability partnership, corporation, and others that can be unique to a particular state. Figure 10.1 lists points to consider when determining the best business structure for your operation.

Figure 10.1: DECIDING ON A BUSINESS STRUCTURE

---

1. Expense. How much does the state charge to register the business. Is there a renewal amount that the state charges every year?

2. Personal Liability. Which business structure provides the level of personal liability you are comfortable with? Do you plan to supplement your personal liability coverage with insurance?

3. Complexity. Are the necessary state forms difficult to complete? Do you need to file them every year?

4. Financing. Are you going to outside sources such as lending institutions or investors to get start-up capital? Will your investors insist on a certain business structure?

5. Taxes. Do you need a specific business structure in order to have a certain tax benefit? Are you planning to place a percentage of your profits back into the business?

6. Growth. Are you planning to hire employees? Is this home-based business a stepping-stone to owning a larger company?

Alert!

File Your Renewal Registration on Time: Most states require that business entities file an annual renewal to keep their business registered. Make sure that you file that renewal by the date required. If you miss this filing date, your state may charge you a hefty fee to be reinstated.

Sole Proprietorship

A *sole proprietorship* is a business that is owned and controlled by one person. Most home-based businesses and other small businesses in the U.S. are sole proprietorships. You do not have to file papers with your state to get permission to create a sole proprietorship. However, you may need to get licenses (professional or occupational) that your state, county, or local government requires.

Most people who choose the sole proprietor option use their own names as the business name. If you choose a different name or a made-up name, your state may require that this new name be registered. Some states call it a *fictitious name* or an *assumed name*, and charge a fee to register this name for you business. Contact your Secretary of State for specific information relating to your situation.

Decision-Making Responsibilities. Management control and decision-making is your responsibility. This gives you maximum freedom to do things your way. You can respond quickly to each day's needs. If you have employees, you are legally responsible for their decisions.

Alert!

Keep Your Customers Informed: A serious problem for any sole proprietor is the possibility of not being available for a given period of time—vacations, business trips, or hospital stays. If you are planning to be away from your business, consider notifying customers of a trip by putting a notice on your voicemail that you are unavailable until a specific date, or running your business remotely using a laptop computer.

Tax Considerations. As a sole proprietor, the Internal Revenue Service (IRS) does not treat you as an employee of your business. You are taxed on all of your net business income at the federal level and in those states with income taxes. All money made by the business, even if you leave it in the business, is taxable.

Personal Liability. In a sole proprietorship, the owner maintains personal liability for all business debts. You can minimize your risks of loss by buying relevant insurance coverage. Such coverage might be for your business property losses, for personal injury, or product liability.

Limited Liability Company

Three benefits of a *limited liability company* (LLC) are:
1. ease of initial filing and annual renewals;
2. same limitation on owner liability as a corporation; and,
3. ability to be taxed as an individual.

Decision-Making Responsibilities. An LLC may be run by one person (as in the sole proprietorship) or have a centralized management structure set up according to the laws of the state. Some states require a board of at least a chief manager and a treasurer. If you are on your own, you can fill both slots.

Currently, the majority of states that recognize an LLC allow it to be run by one person. However, check with the Secretary of State in your locale to determine your specific state requirements.

Other corporation-like features are rules that govern the management. An LLC should have an *operating agreement* that spells out all the rules of the LLC, much like bylaws do for a corporation. (A lawyer familiar with LLC law can help you set up an LLC that will meet your state's laws.)

Tax Considerations. For tax purposes, individuals who own an LLC can ask the IRS to have the business income pass through to the individual owners so they can be taxed as individuals or, the owners can elect to pay corporate taxes, plus pay taxes as individuals. (There actually may be some tax savings if you elect this dual tax system.) Currently, the selection of the dual system allows your LLC to be taxed as a corporation and may require that profits be returned into the LLC. Your accountant can help you decide, based on your operations and goals. Other than the selection of this dual tax system, the LLC has no specific tax considerations and can usually be listed on an individual's annual IRS filing. However, check with your tax preparer or accountant to determine which forms you must file with the IRS. This will be determined by the type of system you are using.

An LLC can combine the tax flexibility of a sole proprietorship with the shareholder liability shield of a corporation. In many states, it is more expensive to start an LLC, but the additional fee expense is worth the liability protection an LLC provides. In order to have a legal LLC, you must follow your state's procedures and criteria for creating one. Otherwise, you risk losing the tax flexibility and limited liability features it offers.

Personal Liability. The liability feature that makes an LLC attractive is that owners (called *members*) are not personally liable for the obligations of the business. However, the owners can destroy this shield of legal protection if they disregard the requirements of the legal structure or if they are personally responsible for wrong-doing.

General Partnerships

A *general partnership* is a business in which each owner/partner owns a percentage of the business. Each owner/partner has a say in the management of the business and works in it. The percentage each owns is designated in the *partnership agreement*. (State laws control the terms that can and cannot be put into a partnership agreement.)

General partnerships are more difficult to organize than a sole proprietorship. Depending on the state, you may need to register your partnership and your partnership agreement using the same type of forms as used in registering corporations.

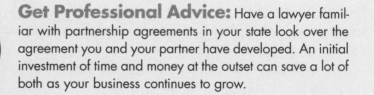

Get Professional Advice: Have a lawyer familiar with partnership agreements in your state look over the agreement you and your partner have developed. An initial investment of time and money at the outset can save a lot of both as your business continues to grow.

Decision-Making Responsibilities. All partners share equally in the responsibilities and rights to manage and control the business. Your agreement and your state's laws may set out some specific requirements. For example, some might require unanimous consent for certain decisions, while other decisions might be allowed by majority vote.

Tax Considerations. While the partnership does not pay federal income tax it still must file certain tax forms every year. The form it must file is Form 1065, *U.S. Partnership Return of Income*. Form 1065 is an *infor-*

mation return that a partnership uses to report its income, deductions, gains, losses, etc. A partnership does not pay tax on its income, but *passes through* any profits or losses to its partners. As stated, partners must then include the partnership items on their tax returns. Other entities that classify itself as partnerships, such as an LLC may, must also file Form 1065.

For each of the individual partners to know what to report as their share of the partnership income (or losses), the partnership must issue a *Schedule K-1*. This form provides the individual partners with the information they need to prepare their individual income tax returns. Partners are liable for tax on their share of the partnership income, whether or not the partnership distributed the income.

If you are involved in a partnership, enlisting the skills of a tax preparer or accountant will be in both the partnerships and your best interest.

Personal Liability. Each general partner is personally liable for the full amount of the partnership's debts. This is true even if a particular partner did not consent to the debt. A well-written partnership agreement can overcome many liability problems. Insurance may also address the extent to which each partner is at risk.

Limited Liability Partnership or Limited Partnership

A *limited liability partnership* (LLP) limits the legal liabilities for business debt to which partnership owners are exposed. (LLPs cannot shield a professional, such as a lawyer, from malpractice claims.) LLPs are tightly governed by the laws of each state—and the laws vary considerably. Most states require that LLPs follow laws that are quite similar to that state's general partnership laws.

Decision-Making Responsibilities. Your partnership agreement can direct who makes the decision in a partnership. Individual state laws may also set out some requirements that must be put into the agreement regarding how decisions are made.

Tax Considerations. Ownership in these kinds of partnerships is divided into shares. You will own the number of shares spelled out in the partnership agreement. To illustrate this, if there were 100 shares total in your partnership agreement and you owned 70 shares in the partnership, then you would own 70% of the partnership. You would then be taxed as an individual on your 70% share of the partnership income. The legal entity—the partnership—is not subject to paying taxes on partnership income because partners already pay income tax on it in their proportional shares.

Personal Liability. In accordance with state laws, an LLP is a partnership that has *two* types of partners. The first is a *general partner*. This type of partner is liable for *all* partnership or business debt. General partners *may* be required to repay business debt by liquidating personal assets. (Most states require a set number of general partners in each LLP.)

The second type is a *limited partner*. This partner invests a specific amount of money into the business. As a result, limited partners are liable *only* for the amount of business debt that is equal to their investment.

Corporation

Some home-based business are structured as *corporations*. This form is usually chosen when the home-based business is run by a group of people or an entire family. Corporations are complex to set up and, depending upon the state, usually required a set of complex actions to renew the corporation each year.

In most states, a corporation is owned by one or more shareholders and is always managed by a board of directors. If there is only one owner, that owner will have to fill at least two offices. Figure 10.2 lists several features of the corporation business structure.

Figure 10.2: FEATURES OF A CORPORATION

A corporation is a legal entity in its own right and is separate and distinct from its owners. For example, the corporation:

- can sue and be sued;
- has tax reporting requirements;
- may need to pay taxes;
- owns all money and property the shareholders will pay to buy stock;
- owns all assets and all money they earn;
- is responsible for all corporate debts and obligations; and,
- must have its own records and a bank account separate from its owners.

The greatest advantage of a corporate form is the protection against personal liability that the corporate owners receive. However, owners are still liable for personal fraud and other fraudulent actions. Figure 10.3 describes the steps used to incorporate a business.

Figure 10.3: START A CORPORATION STEP-BY-STEP

- Choose a name
- Choose a mailing address
- Choose who will be assigned to the corporate titles required by your state
- Follow state laws in creating your Articles of Incorporation, Corporate By-laws, and other documents
- File the proper papers with your state
- Follow the requirements of your state as they relate to arranging meetings and required attendance

---

C Corporations. *C corporations* are the classic type of corporation that many consumers think of when they talk about corporations. The decision-making responsibilities for C corporations rest with the board of directors that manages the affairs of the corporation. The shareholders elect the board. In each of the states, the rules for corporate governance are prescribed by statute. (Decision-making can be more cumbersome than in a sole proprietorship or partnership.)

Tax Considerations for C corporations state that the corporation pays federal and possibly state tax on corporate profits. Remaining profits may be distributed to shareholders as dividends. It establishes its tax year when it files its first income tax return.

S Corporations. *S Corporations* were created to allow small business owners, including home-based owners, to get personal liability protection without having to act like giant business. While they are very much like LLCs, in some states, the LLC for a home-based business gets more benefits than a home-based S Corporation.

Decision-making responsibilities for S corporations can be like owning a sole proprietorship, LLC, or any other corporation. It depends on how your business is set up and the state laws that control S corporations.

Tax considerations include the corporation's income, deductions, and credits as they are passed through to you. Then you pay tax as an individual. An S corporation pays no corporate income tax. (Be sure to check with your lawyer or accountant about your state's requirements for reporting and paying taxes at the state and federal level.)

QUICK Tip

Protection from Personal Liability: The protection against personal liability is one of the major reasons small business owners choose one of the corporate forms.

Nonprofit Corporation

Nonprofit corporations are not often used as a home-based business corporate form. In order to be given the privilege of nonprofit corporate status, the papers filed with your state and the IRS must contain a mission that is approved by your states laws and federal laws as charitable or community-focused. These types of corporations are not businesses in the sense that they earn dividends for their owners or investors. Nonprofits are unique because under federal and state laws, no one is allowed to own them. Instead, their assets are merely held in trust by a board of directors.

Nonprofits are allowed to make a profit if they use that profit for their mission and not to pay compensation to shareholders. Nonprofits are exempt from paying income tax on income received that is related to their charitable or community-focused mission. But they do pay federal income taxes on income received from activities unrelated to their approved mission. (Some states levy property taxes on them, some do not.) Charities are exempt from paying sales tax on items they buy to carry out their approved mission.

(Nonprofit corporations are beyond the scope of this book and if you think you are interested in forming one, you should consult an attorney who has experience in forming them.)

Professional Corporation

Professional corporations are usually limited by most states to licensed members of the same profession. This type of corporation allows professionals to practice in a group of individuals while giving them the same protection from liability as owners of other types of corporations. However, this protection from liability comes with two very big exceptions:

1. a professional corporation must be organized for the sole purpose of rendering professional services and
2. all professionals remain individually liable for their own acts of professional negligence.

If you are a licensed professional and want to consider forming a professional corporation, your state will have information about whether your choice of profession qualifies.

Employer Identification Number

You may want to obtain an EIN or Tax ID number. The IRS assigns an employer identification number (EIN) to identify the tax accounts of most sole proprietors, corporations, partnerships, and employers. If you are a sole proprietor with no employees, the IRS uses your Social Security number as your identification number, however, getting a separate tax ID number may make record keeping easier and cut down on potential identity theft. Banks and other financial institutions will ask you for an EIN. Figure 10.4 describes times an EIN is needed by a business.

Figure 10.4: WHEN DOES MY BUSINESS NEED AN EIN?

You need an EIN for your business if you:

- pay wages to one or more employees;
- operate your business as a corporation or partnership;
- add partners to an existing sole proprietorship, then operate as a partnership; or,
- file returns for employment taxes, excise taxes, or alcohol, tobacco, or firearms taxes.

To get your EIN, you need to fill out IRS *Form SS-4*. You can get the form by contacting the IRS at **www.irs.gov**, calling 800-829-3676, or by going to your local IRS office (and fill out online).

Licenses, Permits, and the Collection of Taxes

When you start a business, you may have to apply and get one or more licenses. Be sure your employees have all of their necessary licenses. You might need to get a license for the business, itself. For example, home-based barber and beauty shops need licenses, and the barbers and stylists need professional licenses. Governments at all levels issue licenses. The federal government, your state, county, and city all may have regulations regarding specific licenses. It is your responsibility to learn what is needed for your business' particular operation.

The majority of business licenses have an expiration date of one year. At that time, you will need to renew the license, and more often than not, pay a renewal fee. Along with annual renewals, your license may have additional requirements. For example in many states, restaurants must be inspected every year; attorneys and doctors need to complete certain courses each year; and, in a retail business, you may need to prove that you complied with laws on collecting taxes for each sale.

Permit and Inspection Requirements

Most local and some county and state governments may want to inspect your home or operations before you open your doors to customers. They may charge an inspection fee. Call your local and county government offices and inquire about permits for the type of operation you plan. If you have to get a permit, you probably will pay a fee when you apply for it. After you get a permit, you may need to have an inspection.

The type of inspections depends on what your operations will be. Health Departments, Public Safety Departments, and Building Safety are just three of the types of inspections that home-based business owners might need to contact. You must contact them and ask them to inspect your business *before you start operating as a business*. Do not wait until they contact you, because they could fine you.

Keep a record of all the permits you obtain, and keep a record of whom you called for an inspection and when you made that call. Should someone try to assess a penalty, you will be able to have evidence that you did all you could to obey the law. (If you have any questions about permits, the permit process, and the inspections, consider consulting your attorney.)

Sales Tax Permit

Before you open your doors, be sure to have all the sales permits that your state requires. If you sell out-of-state, some states, such as Florida, require you to collect their sales tax on items sold to a Florida address. Penalties can be stiff if you do not collect and pay these taxes promptly.

Selling on the Internet: States are interested in finding legal ways to impose sales tax collection responsibilities on businesses that sell online. Be sure your lawyer and accountant keep you updated and prepared to meet these and any other tax liabilities that are imposed upon you.

Local Taxes

You may have to remit taxes to a city, town, or county. Whatever your business activities are, check with the city and the county where you are conducting business to analyze their tax requirements. Like setting up the process you use to collect and remit state sales taxes, be sure to get your permit or paper work done before you even offer to sell one item. If local and county governments have sales taxes, they are often collected and paid by you as part of your state sales tax collection and payment process.

Zoning Regulations

Home-based business owners need to be aware of the zoning laws in their community. Some of the things you need to consider include the following.

- Make sure that your county, city, or town permits you to operate your business from home.
- Find out if your city or town permits you to operate your business the way that you envision.
- Determine if your community's zoning laws allow you to do the type of work you want to do in the location that you have chosen.

If all of these laws favor you—find out what permits are required, how much each permit will cost, how long the permit lasts, and how often you must renew it. You may be able to find the zoning classification in your county, city, or town for your home on the Internet. If not, you will need to get that information from your local government offices. Consult with your attorney if you do not fully understand what the laws and permits require of you.

Do not ignore your local and county zoning laws. If you choose to ignore the laws and your business comes to the attention of government authorities, you could get an order to move or to close your business.

You may live in a type of housing development that requires you to belong to an association (condominium, townhouse, etc.). In that case, you may be subject to additional rules, when running a business from your home. Again, learn those rules and do what it takes to obey them.

If you rent your home, your lease may restrict commercial activity within it. Read your lease closely, to find out if you are permitted to operate a business on your rented property. If the lease is not clear, ask your attorney about the legal and financial risks for operating a business on rental property without the landlord's written consent.

Chapter

Basic Business Setup

From selecting the perfect name for your company to establishing a business account with a local bank; from determining the necessary features of a new computer system to picking the color of your stationery—now is the time to get down to business.

- Naming Your Company
- Bank Account
- Credit Cards
- Telephone Systems
- Computer Hardware
- Computer Software
- Office Equipment
- Tips on Acquiring Equipment and Furniture
- Business Cards, Letterhead, and Envelopes

Naming Your Company

You can name you business almost anything you want, depending on the laws of your state. Review your state's rules as published by your state's Secretary of State. (See the Appendix for Secretary of State information.)

If you are registering your business with a name other than your own full name, you may have to register as an assumed name, fictitious name, or a doing business as (d/b/a) name with your state. Most states require that the other name used for a business is unique and does not imply an affiliation with another known business (if there is no affiliation). That way there is no confusion to the customers about whom they are dealing with.

There may also be restrictions on your choice of names. For example, some states won't let you put a reference to a geographic location in your name unless you are located there. You need to check with your state about its restrictions. Also, some other business already may have that name. You may still be able to use it if you are in a different industry or trade. And you may not be able to use corporate abbreviations if you are a sole proprietor. Some states may allow you to reserve your assumed or fictitious name of choice if you are not quite ready to finalize your choice.

Another consideration is what is common in your industry. For example, gourmet food makers chose names that indicate something good to eat. Each industry has its own practices.

Net-Based Businesses

If you plan to be an Internet-based business or to only have a presence on the Internet, you will also need to choose a domain name. You may want to do some or all of your business over it. You may choose to have only a website filled with information about your product or service. Whichever of these scenarios you choose, you will need to have a domain name.

When selecting a domain name, you will want something that is short and easy to type. Make a list of several domain names that could work for your business. For example, if you are making widgets, **www.widgetbuilder.com**, **www.widgets2go.com**, or **www.USwidgets.com** could be options.

Register Your Domain Name. Next, you will need to make sure that the name is available. If it is available, you will want to immediately register the name for your home-based business. Registering the domain name will require that you pay a monthly fee to keep ownership of the name.

The best way to register a domain name, is to contact one of the many full service, online firms where you can verify that a name is available, apply for registration, and have that online firm host your website. In a recent Google search for "domain names," we came up with over 100,000 hits. These hits represent companies that offer a similar service. You can check to see if your domain name is available on their website (usually without obligation). You can register the name through their website and you can sign up to have this company host your website. The difference is in the services offered.

We found three online firms that are not only very helpful regarding domain name registration, but also provide information on promoting a home-based business website. They are: **www.godaddy.com**, **www.network-solutions.com**, and **www.smallbusiness.yahoo.com**. If all you want to do is check to see if a domain name is available, you can use the website of any of the above listed firms or you can just go to **www.checkdomain.com**. (Keep in mind that just because a domain name is available today that does not mean it will be still available tomorrow.)

Register with Search Engines. While getting the right domain name is important, in order for someone to find your website on the Internet, it is even more important to register your domain name with the best search engines. This gives your site the most exposure. Search engines such as Yahoo or Google provide the public with information about websites on the Internet.

The search engines get this information from businesses, like yours, which register their website under various categories. For example, a law firm might want to register under the categories: law, legal, law firm, personal injury, and lawsuit.

Hosting Your Website. The full service, online firm, such as the ones listed above, register your domain name with the appropriate search engines along with hosting your website on their equipment. Hosting is merely a term for a company that provides the computer equipment where your website resides and where the information regarding your website is stored. This information includes such concerns as the structure of your website, email from customers, orders, and a count of how many people accesses your website. You will pay a fee for hosting, but there are many options that can be tailored to your business.

Bank Account

After you register your business with the state, it is important to get a bank account with the name of the business. Business accounts are usually checking accounts with the official name and address of the business preprinted on the check. Having a business relationship with a local bank can be very beneficial to any home-based business, as bankers can assist you in getting business loans and help you process your revenue. Review Figure 11.1 to identify various services that could be provided by your bank.

Figure 11.1: BANK SERVICES FOR YOUR BUSINESS

Often, home-based businesses make use of bank services more than other types of businesses. These services can be:

- start-up loans;
- tax preparation assistance;
- wire transfer capability;
- direct deposit;
- automatic payment deposits;
- investment accounts;
- savings accounts; and,
- retirement account products.

Be sure to account for the charges of each bank service you use in your budget.

Find a Banking Partner: Beware of banks that focus on loans, but do not seem to understand that a business has many other needs. You may have to go to several banks and ask about the specific services you want in order to locate the best bank for your new business.

Internet Services

Many home-based business owners will like a bank's Internet services, such as the ability to pay bills online. Banks have excellent Internet security. However, at this early stage in home-computer security development, you may risk theft of identity and funds when you use Internet banking. Consider the risks if you choose convenience over safety.

Business Checking Account

Your basic banking need at the outset is for a checking account. This is an important item in your business future. Find out the exact costs your bank will charge for having a business account. The fees tend to be more than for personal accounts. Banks often charge for deposits, checks you write, and those you receive into your account. Many banks' fee structures are based on the dollar volume of your transactions.

Overdraft charges can be expensive. Under new regulations, banks can decrease the time you have to get money into your account to cover withdrawals. Many banks offer a protection from the high charges associated with an overdraft for a low, monthly, flat fee. Understand your bank's policies and charges so that you can plan accordingly.

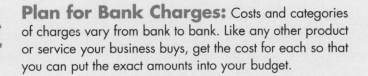

Plan for Bank Charges: Costs and categories of charges vary from bank to bank. Like any other product or service your business buys, get the cost for each so that you can put the exact amounts into your budget.

Credit Cards

When you open your home-based business, you need to decide if you are going to accept credit card payments. There are two reasons not to accept credit cards—your industry does not normally use them, and it will cost you a percentage of the sale to accept a credit card in payment from a customer.

There are some industries that just normally do not use the credit card option. This is especially true when you are providing a service to another business. For example, the cleaning crew who nightly maintains an office, does not end every night with the question, "Will this be cash or credit?" This type of service is normally billed to the business on a weekly, biweekly, or monthly basis.

Many small businesses do not realize that by accepting credit cards for payment that they must pay a percentage of that payment back to the credit card company. In addition to the percentage of the sale, some credit card companies also charge businesses for the equipment used to swipe the credit card. In some cases, the business is also charged for the access time required to get a computer approval on a transaction.

QUICK Tip

Know the Cost of Taking Credit Cards: Before you sign up with any company offering to set you up to accept credit cards, know your cost. For some businesses that price their products at the lowest possible amount, even a small percentage to the credit card company can be a problem.

Telephone Systems

Identify the characteristics that you want in a telephone system then determine which of the many features available will be worth your money. Not only are there specific features available on certain telephones, but there are different features available as part of your phone service.

So, how do you figure out what you need? Well, you could hire a high-priced communications consultant that has probably never actually run a business like yours. You could talk to the telephone company whose interest is in selling you as many services as possible. You could talk to other business owners that are running home-based businesses with missions similar to yours. However, you know more about your own needs than anyone does.

QUICK Tip

Envision Your Daily Tasks: This is a good time to walk yourself through the business you are planning to go into—step-by-step. Imagine each day. Imagine the various scenarios that may arise. Think about the part the telephone could play in each.

Land-Based Telephones

What you need in a land phone will depend a lot on how you use it in your business. A gourmet caterer that delivers will have different needs than an accountant who communicates with clients mostly in person, via email, or by mail. Figure 11.2 describes particular features and benefits of various telephone options.

Figure 11.2: CONSIDER VARIOUS TELEPHONE FEATURES

Think about your business's unique needs as you consider the following telephone features:

- hands-free speakerphone (handy when you have to feed your baby while you talk);
- multiple line phones (if you can afford them, so you do not tie up your home phone line);
- automatic redial (lets you use one hand to dial the phone, while pulling the client's file with the other hand);
- programmable memory (saves time by putting all commonly-called numbers in one location so you do not waste time looking up the number repeatedly);
- caller identification capability (allows the opportunity to decide if you want to stop working to answer the phone call of a chatty friend or family member); and,
- mute capability (very helpful when your family is being noisy).

There are many basic features available as part of your telephone service, such as: voice mail, call waiting, call forwarding, call parking, and conference calling. Once you have determined the telephone features that will be needed, it is time to make the decision about a long-distance service provider. Given the competition, prices have never been better. This is also true for toll-free numbers. Due to the low cost, home businesses can now afford this valuable customer benefit.

Cell Phones

Cell phone technology is evolving rapidly. Cell phones now do all the things that land-based phones do (caller ID, call-waiting, call forwarding, etc.), and more. You need to learn as much as possible about the wireless technology that supports cell phones and make the best choice for your business. On one hand, you may need a cell phone that simply permits clients to reach you when you are out of the office. On the other hand, you may need a cell phone that will allow you to access the Internet and send emails.

Ensure Customer Satisfaction: If you intend to rely on a cell phone for all your business calls, make sure that the cell phone has excellent reception. Your home-based business may be viewed as less than serious if your calls sound like they are coming from a tin-can; your phone frequently drops calls; or, if your calling area is so limited that you lose calls.

Service Providers

As you choose a service provider, be sure to evaluate each vendor's quality of service in the areas in which you plan to do business. It may make more sense for you to have two separate cell phone service providers. If you are located in a rural area, a local provider may offer more economical and reliable service, whereas if you have to travel, a separate, national service provider may be a better bet. Your combined cost may, in fact, be lower than paying roaming charges on just one plan.

There are numerous cell phone service providers. Much like with land phones, each provider offers countless plans. The good news is that the competition continues to drive down prices. The bad news is that the plans change frequently. It is hard to evaluate absolutely everything when the technology and plans are changing so fast. However, try to project your needs into the future. Make a vendor decision you can easily live with in order to save the time-consuming hassle of shopping around.

Computer Hardware

If telephone technology is developing rapidly, computer technology is evolving at lightning speed. The good news is that prices keep coming down. The bad news is that it is difficult to keep up with the changing technology. When you buy a new computer system, new standards and features emerge almost before you get oriented to the system you just purchased. How do you figure out what you need? Figure 11.3 lists some questions that need to be answered as you consider purchasing computer equipment.

Figure 11.3: QUESTIONS TO ASK ABOUT SPECIFIC HARDWARE

- Which platform (MAC or PC) is best for your business?
- Do you need a portable system (laptop)?
- What do want in a keyboard?
- What kind of CD drive do you need?
- What will you use to back up your data?
- What other types of hardware will you need in addition to the computer?

If the prospect of purchasing a computer makes your eyes glaze over, take heart. In the course of your life, you have bought many machines without understanding exactly how they work—washers and dryers, automobiles, snow blowers, stereo systems, etc. What you have known when you bought those machines was what you needed and wanted them to do for you. That is what you will need to decide before buying your computer. Use the same approach you use for the other machines. Shop around. Get yourself educated. Read computer magazines and books. Visit the computer stores and talk to techies. Gradually you will begin to acquire a basic understanding and develop a sense of what you need.

Platform

If you plan to share or exchange files regularly with other businesses, you might be wise to explore whether they are using Macs or PCs. While, many software programs can convert files created in another platform, it is still simpler for a Mac to talk to a Mac and a PC to talk to a PC.

Alert!

Check Your Industry Standard: Some industries tend to favor one platform over another. For example, most software that has been developed for the legal industry is written for the Windows platform and is designed to run on a PC. Very few legal software programs are written for Macs.

You call tell what type of platform (Mac or Windows) an industry favors by looking at what kind of software the industry requires. All software will indicate if it is written for a Macintosh computer or Windows. While this has been a problem for some businesses in prior years, we are now seeing more software programs being written for both types of platforms.

Portability

A few years ago, portability was probably a bigger issue that it is today. Back then, if you needed to leave your home with your computer, you might have purchased a laptop and a desktop system. Today, laptop or notebook computers can serve both purposes. Notebook and laptop computers have a PC card slot. It lets you insert a credit-card sized expansion card. You then can add features, functions, and devices. You can use your notebooks or laptops on the road. When you get back home, you just plug them into a connection port that is hooked up to your other external peripherals (components). Once plugged in, the laptop serves as the brains for the desktop system. This eliminates the need for a desktop computer.

If you need something even more portable than a laptop, you may be a candidate for a hand held electronic device such as a palmtop, a personal digital assistant (PDA), or a personal information manager (PIM). Features vary, but include many of the same features as a desktop or laptop system. An infrared or cable connection allows you to exchange information with your desktop or laptop system, as well as with another palm-sized device.

Brand

The computer you choose should depend upon which company provides the best technical support. The last thing you want to do is save money on a computer and then allocate time in your schedule to be on the phone waiting and waiting for help setting up or maintaining that system. The quality of a company's technical support division depends on the company employees answering your phone calls. Those employees can be affected by many factors. These factors range from whether you can communicate your concerns accurately to whether there are enough of them to answer all of the calls. Because employee performance can change over time, the identity of the company with the best technical support can also change over time. Investigate your options and come to your own conclusion.

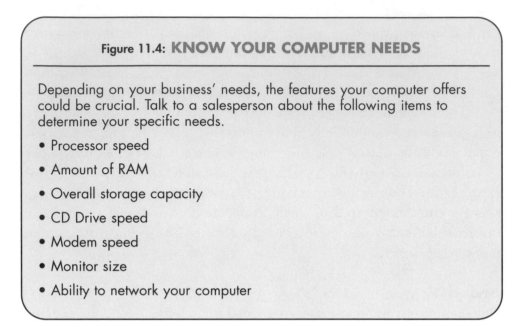

Figure 11.4: **KNOW YOUR COMPUTER NEEDS**

Depending on your business' needs, the features your computer offers could be crucial. Talk to a salesperson about the following items to determine your specific needs.

• Processor speed

• Amount of RAM

• Overall storage capacity

• CD Drive speed

• Modem speed

• Monitor size

• Ability to network your computer

Keyboards

Remember to think about a keyboard when you shop for your computer. While it often comes bundled with the purchase, a keyboard is a personal thing. Different keyboards have a unique feel. (Bundled means you cannot pick the keyboard.)

In addition, the repetitive wrist, hand, and finger motion used in keyboard stroking has caused injuries for some people, including carpal tunnel syndrome. If you have a history of such injuries or are prone to such injuries, consider some of the newer, ergonomically designed keyboards that involve hand positioning supposedly designed to minimize injuries. Keyboard choice is really a matter of personal comfort and injury prevention.

CD Drives

Most computer software is now distributed on CD (compact disc), so you will need a CD drive for your computer. Almost all computers come with a built-in CD drive, however, an external CD drive can be added to an existing system if need be. Most CD drives are CD-RW drives that read and write on the CDs. (The term that has become more popular for writing to a CD is burning.)

CD-RWs can also serve a very important function for your computer system. You can use them to back up your data. (CD-RWs can be reused, similar to the old floppy discs.) *The most important thing is to remember to back up your data.*

Modems

A modem is a technological device that links with the Internet and other computers or fax machines via telephone lines. A modem allows you to gain access to the Internet and send or receive a fax. Modem quality is a function of speed.

Other technologies include cable, digital subscriber lines (DSL), or T1 lines. These usually create faster connections than do most modems. While DSL is faster than access through a regular dial modem, it still uses the telephone lines. Cable is becoming more widely available and is often more affordable than DSL. This is particularly true if you already subscribe to cable television. T1 lines are the fastest type of connection. They are ideal for selling over the Internet. They are also the most expensive. Unless your business is dependent on Internet sales, it may be unnecessary.

One other important distinction between the various types of connections is whether you need to dial up to establish the connection each time you want to go online or whether the connection is constant. With a regular modem and DSL, you must dial up and establish a connection before you can transmit information. Although brief, you encounter a delay while the connection is established. With cable and T1 lines, the connection is constant so there is no need to dial up. You can transmit immediately.

Monitors

Much like keyboards, monitors often come bundled in a computer package. Monitor quality is consistent enough to make it difficult to comparison shop based on quality alone. The size of the screen is often the most important variable. While a 15-inch monitor may be usable, you will appreciate a 17-inch monitor if you sit at your computer for long periods during your business day. Flat screen and LCD monitors are becoming more affordable and popular. In addition, a flat screen monitor takes up significantly less space on the top of your desk.

Networks

If you will work with at least one other person with whom you want to share data or an external peripheral (like a printer), then a network may be your best option. If you are considering a network, depending on whom you network with, you may need to examine your data. If you have privacy concerns, then categorize it as either nonprivate or private. Private data is information such as employee performance evaluations, payroll information, and intellectual property matters such as trade secrets.

Alert!

Private and Not Private Data: Do not network the data you consider private. This way you can eliminate the danger of it being viewed by unauthorized users.

Networks can be set up for two purposes: to share files and to allow multiple users to connect to the Internet through a single connection. As long as Internet Service Provider (ISP) prices continue to rise, rather than fall, a network can prove to be a substantial savings for your business.

Printers

A printer is one of the single most important components of any computer system. Printer technology, just like processor technology, continues to advance at an incredible speed. A small business owner can now afford a laser printer or an ink-jet printer that produces photograph-quality color documents. Ink jet printers lay down microscopic dots of ink to produce a printed document. Because ink is actually involved, the copy can smear. Laser printers use an ink-to-light process to produce an image, so there is no ink to smear.

Quality of Document Production. As you compare printers, you will run into measurement terms that allow you to compare the quality of documents produced by each printer. DPI (dots per inch) is the measure of resolution. It refers to how crisp and clear the print looks. The faster the dpi, the better the resolution is. However, the quality of paper can also have an impact on the resolution. Since laser printers use light rather than ink process to print, dpi is not relevant if you are considering a laser printer.

Speed, measured by pages per minute (ppm), is relevant for both ink-jet and laser printers. Historically, laser printers have produced the darkest, sharpest quality text. Today's ink-jet printers are not far behind. Laser printers have also historically had faster ppm speeds. But there is a short delay before the first page begins printing. Visit a computer store or big box office supply store to test the various printers to see which type works best for your business.

Scanners

If you will need to copy preexisting documents into your computer so that you can edit or manipulate text or graphics, then you will need a scanner. Scanner quality is also measured by dots per inch. This measurement reflects how much detail the scanner picks up. Scanners use special software that determines the amount of detail your scanned document will contain.

Miscellaneous Computer Add-ons

As always seems to be the case when you are shopping for something, the list of computer add-ons or extras is endless. Consider a few that make good business sense.

Sudden power outages can cause devastating results, so you should not be without an *uninterruptible power supply* (UPS). (If you have ever spent a lot of time and energy creating a document, only to lose it in an instant when the power went out, you probably already own a UPS.)

A *surge protector* is another electrical device that provides additional places to plug in other computer components. Most importantly, it protects your system from destruction in the event of lightning or other power surge.

You may want a *wrist rest* for your keyboard and mouse. Do this if you are prone to the repetitive type injuries associated with frequent keyboard use. Similarly, a *non-glare screen cover* will ease the strain on your eyes.

Computer Software

The best computer system is only as good as the software loaded onto it. You want to maximize the benefits of your computer. To do this, invest some time to determine what type of software will best suit your business needs. Software changes as rapidly as hardware. So before you buy, make sure you educate yourself about the latest products on the market. Read the latest reviews in the computer magazines. Visit the computer shows. Talk to software vendors.

Get Reliable Information about Computer Software: Talk to people who use the programs you are considering buying. Other business owners in your industry or profession may be the best source of information regarding specific software.

Computer Support

More importantly, you will want to check into the technical support available with each program. Just as with hardware, the technical support feature may be more important than anything. This is particularly true if you are inexperienced.

Invest Money to Make Money: The professional version of QuickBooks software is a favorite among tax accountants, however, there are many versions available for the small business. Check out their website at **www.quickbooks.com** or visit an office supply store. While QuickBooks has products that can help you with everything from bill collection to inventory to a credit card system, evaluate the various brands that are available. Invest in one that provides only the features you need for your business.

Once you make your purchase, consider attending one of the many software training sessions available. They are usually available either through the place you made your purchase, a private organization, or local educational institution. Training can make you proficient with your software quickly.

Alert!

Register Your Software: Register your software as soon as you purchase it. Usually the program will prompt you to do so as you install it. Registering the software allows the manufacturer to record you as the legitimate owner who is entitled to technical support. (When people copy software purchased by others (bootlegged software) they are not entitled to technical support.)

Manufacturers typically have a technical support function available through their website. Most will also have telephone technical support. It is always a good idea to attempt to get your questions answered through the website or by emailing the technical support department. (While sometimes necessary, telephoning a technical support representative often proves frustrating.)

There are many types of software. All systems should have some type of software that protects against computer viruses and allows for file back-up. It is also hard to imagine any business that can exist without word processing software. Depending on your business, there may be other specialized software that you will need to be successful.

Stamps.com

A terrific product for any business, especially for a home-based business, is Stamps.com. You can get the software off the Internet or from some office supply stores. With **www.stamps.com** you are able to print your return address, your sender's name/address, and postage on an envelope of almost any size or on a label. (This software also allows printing individual stamps for those pre-addressed envelopes.) You can send items with insurance, first class, return signature required, express, priority, or any other way that the

U.S. Post Office allows. For those services that require additional forms, you will need to get them from your local post office.

There are several pluses for using this software. The primary one is being able to apply postage and a dated postmark to an item after the local post office has closed. No more driving like crazy to the post office just before it closes because the item you are sending must be postmarked before today.

This software allows you to create a library of names and addresses of people you mail items to. You only enter the name and address once. Imagine the time saving if your business sends out monthly bills to the same people month after month. This library becomes you master list of customers and it can be imported into a file used by word processing software.

QUICK Tip

Proof of Mailing: Stamps.com allows you to produce reports on items you have applied postage to. If someone says you didn't mail him or her something, you run a report and have a record of the shipment.

Stamps.com does charge a monthly fee, but once you begin to use it you will see it is well worth it. You can also purchase supplies such as labels, postage scales, etc. from them. This is a must have for any home business.

Office Equipment

Besides the basic office equipment, there are other office machines that can become essential to running your business efficiently. These machines can offer you another way to communicate with customers, plus give you the ability to operate the business faster.

Fax Machines

Just as it is hard to imagine a business without a telephone or computer, it is hard to imagine a business without a fax machine. Fax machines have become standard for many home business operations.

If your computer has a fax board, you can receive and send faxes via your computer. The copy on computer faxes is clearer and crisper because you bypass the distortions created during the scanning process involved in transmitting from fax machine to fax machine. However, there are some drawbacks. You do need to have your computer on and in standby mode to receive a computer fax. If you leave your computer running continually rather than power down each night, that may not be much of a problem. Of course, that practice might run up your electric bill.

There is another limitation—unless you have a scanner as part of your system, a computer fax can only transmit computer files. A standard fax machine can transmit handwritten notes, copies of pictures or articles from a magazine or newspaper—even handprints.

Despite the computer related alternatives available to standard fax technology, fax machines will endure. Just as the computer did not replace the need for storage of printed documents, email and computer fax boards will not replace the need for fax machines. You will need to figure out what technological devices accomplish your business goals in the manner best suited to your operations at home and arrange your resources accordingly.

You will need to decide if you want a dedicated phone line for your fax machine or whether you are willing to have your fax and phone share a line. If you plan to use one line for both, you definitely want a fax machine that has an automatic phone/fax switch. That feature will automatically direct faxes to the fax machine without the caller needing to do anything special.

Use Your Fax Machine, Efficiently: If you regularly receive or send faxes, you will find it beneficial to invest in a second phone line. If not, pay a small monthly fee to your local telephone company for a distinctive ring-tone feature.

Photocopiers

Photocopiers have been around for a long time. While affordable machines are available, prices are not declining as rapidly as with other office equipment. Multifunction machines (described in the next section) can perhaps reduce the overall cost even more.

If you are considering whether to postpone purchasing a copier until your business is up and running, think about the alternatives. Measure the cost of making copies at a local copy shop in dollars, time, and convenience. If it is convenient, you have time to spare in your schedule, and your needs are minimal, perhaps it makes sense. If the closest place to make copies is twenty-five miles away and you need to make hundreds of copies several times a week, the cost of an in-home machine might make more "cents."

Once you decide that you need a copier, determine the kind of copier that will best serve your operation. First, just like with printers, you need to compare copiers. That means knowing how copy quality is defined. Copy speed is measured in copies per minute. Copy reliability is measured by how many copies your machine will make before you need to call the copy repairperson to fix it. As with many purchases (but certainly not all), if you buy a more expensive copier, you can expect to get more copies. In other words, you get greater reliability before you have to pay for service.

If your copy needs will be minimal you can likely get by with a personal copier that will fit on the top of your desk. It will cost a few hundred dollars. If your business copies hundreds or thousands of copies per month, then you may be in the market for a much more sophisticated and expensive machine. (Remember, this machine will be one that takes up lots more space.) Review the questions in Figure 11.5 to prepare for the purchase of a copier.

Figure 11.5: QUESTIONS TO ASK ABOUT PHOTOCOPIERS

The following are some questions to consider when searching for a copier.

- Do you want your copier to sort and collate documents?

- Do you need to copy multiple sized documents?

- Do you want a copier that can feed a stack of documents rather than a single sheet?

- Do you need a copier that will fold, staple, and bind?

- Do you need to make two-sided copies?

- Do you want to be able to enlarge or reduce documents that you copy?

- How often are you willing to load the paper trays?

- Do you want a copier that will automatically switch from an empty to a full paper tray?

Multifunction Machines

If you will be able to get by with a basic copier, you may want to consider a multifunction machine. These four-in-one machines print, scan, copy, and fax. Most fax machines have a copy feature. But the quality of the copies made using that feature varies. True multifunction machines produce much better copy.

If you will operate your business in a confined space—perhaps a converted closet or nursery, a multifunction machine may be very desirable. It takes up considerably less space than a separate printer, scanner, copier, and fax machine.

Tips on Acquiring Equipment and Furniture

Perhaps you already have some or all of the equipment you need. Make business judgments about what you want to use your equipment for—

the capabilities your current equipment has, and the gaps that you need to fill. Determine if your current equipment and furniture need updating or modification.

If you need to buy equipment, the first thing to do is price what you want and then prepare a budget for all items. Prioritize each of the items based on when you estimate you will need them, plus, a guess as to when you will be able to afford them.

New vs. Used

When you need to purchase equipment or furniture, you have the option of buying new or used. Your local office or computer supply store is a good place to start when looking for new items. However, used office equipment is also readily available. You can find reputable dealers through the Yellow Pages, newspaper advertisements, word-of-mouth, or other business resources in your location. You can also find new or used equipment on the Internet, either through dealers or online auctions. (Often you will find the best prices online so you may want to shop locally to educate yourself and then comparison shop online before making a purchase.)

Be sure to consider warranties and repair or service agreements when you shop. With computer equipment, the technology is advancing so rapidly you are likely to be in the market for new equipment before anything has a chance to break down or need repair. Despite that, make sure you know what guarantees you are buying—no matter what you are buying. The same goes for extended service agreements. (Often these "add-on" products are priced to make money for the seller.)

Leasing

Leasing equipment and furniture may be another option for you. Although vehicles may be the first thing that comes to mind when you think of leasing and business, you can lease just about anything. With electronic equipment or technology, one advantage to leasing may be the ability to exchange outdated equipment as new technology emerges.

QUICK Tip

Understand the Leasing Terms: Operations that sell equipment often lease it, too. Check the leasing agreement very carefully. Make sure you understand the terms. Depending on your business and the type of leasing deal involved, you may want to have your attorney review it.

As a new business owner, you may find it difficult to lease because your business has no credit history. Depending on the size and nature of your business, leasing in your own name may be an option. (This means you will need to have a positive, personal credit history.)

Business Cards, Letterhead, and Envelopes

If you have a business, no matter how small, you will need business cards, letterhead, and envelopes. However, you do not have to pay a fortune for a professional look.

Business cards are extremely important. They are a marketing tool, a referral tool, and can be used for short notes to potential customers and/or vendors. As you network (talking to another person about your business), you are bound to be asked for your business card. Keep a supply of business cards with you at all times, ready to hand out.

If you have a good printer you can print your own business cards. Business card paper stock, already perforated, is available at most office supply stores. You can also get good deals on business cards through vendors on the Internet, those that advertise in the Sunday papers, and your local print shop. Business cards do not have to be fancy or have special printing (unless your market demands such trappings).

Letterhead is the second most important component to your professional image. You need letterhead for invoices, for bids on certain jobs, to introduce your business to potential customers, and a myriad of other business correspondence.

You can create your own letterhead on your computer, especially if you are adept at manipulating fonts and have a good printer. In some word processing software you can even create a macro (group of instructions) that automatically puts your specialized letterhead on your correspondence. For those who are either not adept, or who do not want to spend the time figuring it out, there are local print shops and office supply stores that have print departments.

In contrast to the emphasis you need to put into getting printed letterhead, save yourself money and do not get your return address printed on envelopes. To most, envelopes are rather meaningless. They need to hold your contents, provide space for a clear address, and contain the proper postage—that is all.

Chapter

Use Business Experts to Your Advantage

In addition to yourself, there are at least three other people that play a significant role in the success of your home-based business: your attorney, your accountant, and your insurance agent.

▶ **The Attorney**

▶ **The Accountant**

▶ **The Insurance Agent**

▶ **Business Records**

The Attorney

In the early days of your business, various legal issues will surface and you will find it beneficial to work with an attorney. If you are not already working with an attorney, it will be helpful to know how to find a lawyer who is suitable for your needs.

Treat the search for a lawyer as you would the one for the right employee or partner—with preparation, care, and thought. Your goal should be to find at least three lawyers to interview. If you live in a rural community, you may not have that many to choose from. General practitioners in rural communities are often skilled in many areas of the law, including small business matters. If they do not feel confident in representing you, ask for a referral.

Finding an Attorney

A person who is starting a home-based business needs to work with an attorney who is experienced in small business start-ups. These types of attorneys are also labeled as concentrating in Business Law or in Incorporation Law. Make sure the lawyer you select has experience in dealing with small home-based businesses. Those attorneys who only deal with large conglomerates and huge corporations may not be able to adequately assist a small business owner.

Choosing an attorney, for any reason, can be confusing. Many people rely on referrals from family, friends, or business associates such as your banker, insurance broker, or accountant. Other sources for attorney referrals are local bar associations, national bar associations, Internet legal sites, phone books, and by Internet research. Review the Internet sites in Figure 12.1. These will provide a good place to begin an Internet search for an attorney.

Figure 12.1: ATTORNEY REFERRAL WEBSITES

One of the largest bar associations you can contact for a referral is the national American Bar Association at **www.abanet.org**. There are also several legal Internet sites that can also provide you with an attorney referral. Some of the most common are the following.

- www.alllaw.com
- www.lawyers.com
- www.martindale.com
- www.attyfind.com
- www.law4usa.org
- www.findlaw.com
- www.lawyerbureau.com
- www.legal-database.com

Working with an Attorney

Before you decide on whom you will hire to do your legal work, you will want to determine what some of that work will be. Begin by making a list of all the legal topics you think you might need help with. (Figure 12.2 is a good place to start.) Be as specific as you can. Write out every possible question. Include on your list the legal issues you discover as you work on your start-up activities. Then, prioritize your list of legal needs.

Figure 12.2: COMMON LEGAL CONCERNS

Some of the most common legal concerns include the following:

- legal issues you think will arise in your business based on your goals and your mission;
- best business entity (legal form) for your goals;
- current tax laws that will affect you and your business;
- licenses and other business permits you will need;

continued

- contract requirements;

- legal aspects of a franchise you may be considering;

- employment policies and procedures for conformity to all relevant laws;

- overall legality of your business and its mission in relation to local laws and regulations;

- liability risks that will be specific to your operations; and,

- intellectual property rights you will or do own regarding a trademark, service mark, patent, copyright, or trade secrets.

Keeping Legal Costs Down

At the first meeting with an attorney, be honest about your ability to pay and the limits of your budget. A good attorney will welcome your honesty and be glad to provide you with an approximation of legal costs up front. If your attorney does not feel this way or you do not feel comfortable with this person, find another lawyer. In most areas you have lots of choices for legal representation.

One way to keep legal costs down is to be prepared for all meetings with your attorney. This means you need to do some research so that you can ask the right questions. Do not wait until the last minute to gather information—get copies of documents and write out your list of questions.

Prepare for Your Attorney Meeting: Take notes during your meeting with your attorney. A well-prepared client who comes to meetings ready to work conveys a message that he or she will not pay for wasted time.

Your First Meeting

When you set up an initial meeting with an attorney, you may be asked to bring specific documents, general information, and possibly a check for the initial consultation fee (not all attorneys charge consultation fees). Make sure that you understand and can provide the most current documents and information requested. If you decide to meet with an attorney who requires an initial consultation fee, please remember to bring the check with you.

Your attorney will ask you specific financial information—respond honestly. Information given to your attorney is held in confidence by law. Discuss your business objectives and your concerns about your new business. Listen to what your attorney advises. If you do not understand, insist on clarification. (Many attorneys, especially those in small firms, started out just as you are now. They may be able to provide you with the benefits of their actual experience.)

Above all, if you do hire an attorney, follow your attorney's advice. Clients who ask their attorney for advice and then do not follow it are wasting both time and money. There is nothing more frustrating or more detrimental to a good attorney-client relationship than a client who acts against the attorney's direction and then expects the attorney to fix the mess.

Contracting with an Attorney

After you decide if you are going to hire a small business lawyer (and possibly an intellectual property lawyer), be sure that each lawyer develops a written agreement that allows the lawyer to represent you. In some states, it is unethical for lawyers to work without a written agreement. Even if it is ethical in your state, an unwritten agreement invites potential dispute.

The rate or flat fee the lawyer will charge must be in the agreement. If the lawyer wants to be paid in stock, think long and hard about it. Stock gives its owner voting rights. Do you want that? In some states, that may not be ethical for a lawyer to do. (The need to protect the value of his or her stock versus your business needs may be a conflict of interest for the lawyer.)

Be cautious regarding the lawyer you choose for the legal representation. This is about your business. You must be able to trust your lawyer. This professional should be a comfort to you, not a hassle or a hazard. The relationship from legal service delivered to accurate billing and your payment should flow smoothly.

QUICK Tip

Dealing with Your Attorney: The minimum standard for judging your relationship with a lawyer should be the quality of the communication between the two of you. At the very least—it should be excellent.

Many people go into business and decide not to work with a lawyer. They often encounter legal problems when they start this way, which costs both time away from the business and thousands of dollars lost unnecessarily. Spending a little money up front on legal advice often prevents catastrophes later. There are times when legal and other professional help is definitely in your best interest as a new business owner.

The Accountant

A small business accountant can be of great help to you in your early days when you have to set up your business' books. An accountant can help you design a bookkeeping system tailored to your needs; identify your tax paying obligations and a system to pay them; and, help you to identify correct ways to categorize income and expenses. One of the most valuable contributions your accountant can make is to help you determine the financial health of your business.

Like lawyers, accountants are highly credentialed professionals. You want to choose one whose credentials and experience show he or she knows how to work with small businesses. Those who work only with Fortune 500-size corporations, have spectacular credentials, but may not have the skills to work with someone of your size and with your needs.

Check on the status of any licenses they have. If an accountant claims to be a certified public accountant, ask to see his or her certificate. Most accountants are pleased to have someone take an interest in their qualifications because they are proud of having put in many years of energy and education to achieve their expertise.

How an Accountant Can Help You at the Outset

An accountant can help you design an accounting system tailored to your operations. An efficient system that encompasses current practices and standards can be valuable for your small business. Such a system allows you to have an orderly method to keep track of your financial picture. It ties together the marketing and management operations of your business. The information in Figure 12.3 identifies specific benefits of a good accounting system.

Figure 12.3: EFFICIENT ACCOUNTING SYSTEM BENEFITS

You should be able to use your accounting system to:

- collect data;
- organize data;
- maintain data;
- file financial reports;
- give useful information to bankers and creditors;
- have at hand the information you need to operate your business in a profitable and efficient way;
- make the tax-preparation process efficient; and,
- structure your transactions for the lowest tax liability.

QUICK Tip

Business vs. Personal Finances: A good accounting system is necessary to help the new, home-based business owner differentiate business income and expenses from personal financial matters. Depending upon your business structure, this may not be a "nice thing to have"—it may be necessary in order to conform with legal regulations.

A few long-term accounting practices have changed due to recent corporate scandals. Working with a competent small business accountant will help you run your business legally and honorably.

Accounting Methods

Your accountant may ask you questions to determine which of the two principal accounting methods will be appropriate for your operations—cash or accrual. An accounting method is a set of rules used to determine when and how income and expenses are reported. You and your accountant will have to make a decision by the time you file your federal income tax (at the latest).

Your accounting system is not a place for opinions or guesses. It is a place for facts. Recent business scandals and the resulting criminal convictions publicly revealed that accounting techniques can be abused and manipulated. They can be made to show a false picture of how things are. Business persons that are ethical will stay away from these activities. The honest ones will carefully avoid anyone who would lead them into any of these situations.

The method you use for your accounting system will depend upon the size and complexity of your business. If you can afford it, at minimum pay an accountant to set up your books so you can keep your business records accurate.

Cash Method. Cash methods only means two things. First, that all of the gross income you receive is recorded in the year that you receive it. Second, that your expenses are accounted for in the year in which you spend the money. (Cash method does not mean that you accept only cash in exchange for your goods or services.)

QUICK Tip

Cash Only: The easiest accounting method to work with is the cash method. Sole proprietors often use it. This is especially true if they do not carry inventory.

CASE STUDY: Cash Accounting Method

Bill runs an independent secretarial service for a dozen small businesses in his home state. He sent out his monthly invoices at the end of November. He received payment from ten businesses before December 31ˢᵗ, 2005. He declared that income in the year he received it, 2005. He received the last two payments in early January 2006. He will have to put those checks into his 2006 books.

On June 1, 2006, Bill bought a subscription to his local newspaper at the annual rate of $160.00. It was less expensive than shorter subscription rates. The newspaper allowed him to spread his annual payments and bills, quarterly. The newspaper automatically bills his credit card company $40.00 every three months.

In the year 2006 (the year that Bill started the subscription), he enters the $40.00 cost in his books on the date he pays his credit card statement. Bill pays his credit card bill on the 26ᵗʰ of the month.

Since he is billed quarterly, Bill pays $40.00 on June 26ᵗʰ, September 26ᵗʰ, and December 26ᵗʰ, 2005. This means that he will have paid $120.00 for his newspaper subscription in 2006. In 2006, he enters the three payments of $40.00. He will have a $120.00 publication deduction on his taxes for 2006.

Accrual Method. Another way to keep books is the accrual accounting method. If you carry inventory, you must use this method. Under this method, you report income in the year you earn the money. (It does not matter when you receive it.) Accounting for expenses under the accrual method can be tricky. You indicate the expense in your books if three events have occurred:

- your liability is fixed;
- your liability can be determined; and,
- you have paid your liability.

CASE STUDY: Accrual Accounting Method

John produces electronic widgets. The product contains 275 individual parts that John's employees assemble and modify for customers. John's inventory consists of a supply of each of one the 275 parts, some parts pre-assembled into groups, and fully-assembled widgets without modification. Because John has inventory, he must use the accrual method of accounting as directed by his accountant.

Last year, during the month of November, John's business received fifty orders for widgets. Thirty of the orders were for widgets without modification. These thirty orders are filled right away, shipped, and billed before December 1. Under the accrual method, the thirty orders that were shipped and billed were recorded as earned income on the business books in the year they were billed. It does not matter that none of the thirty customers paid John until well into the next year.

Twenty of the fifty customers ordered widgets with modifications that ranged from simple assembly issues to needing another special part. As the special part was purchased, it was paid for and became an expense of the business. Nineteen of these orders did not become earned income until the modified widgets were sent to the customer and billed, which occurred the year following receipt of the original orders.

The exception to this situation was for one customer who ordered specialty part. This customer prepaid his order. Here the money was received first in one year, but due to waiting for that part and the extra time needed to get the assembly right, the part was not shipped until the next year. In this case, the earned income was recorded in the year it was received.

Choose the Correct Accounting Method: Do not use the accrual method of accounting for a noninventory business without the advice of an experienced, small business accountant. There may be IRS problems if your business uses one accounting method and in a future year wants to change to different methods.

Taxes

The main ongoing issue that your accountant will handle is taxes. After dealing with the initial tax related matter of your new business, your accountant can help you keep up with the requirements of the various business tax systems.

Alert!

Develop a Tax Payment System Early: It is critical to have a tax payment system for your business that:

- is appropriate to your situation;
- is valid for the states where you do business;
- reflects the type and amount of income your business earns; and,
- works with the business entity you have chosen.

Income Tax. If you have net profits, you must pay taxes. All of your valid business expenses get deducted from the income (revenue) your business earns (your gross income). Your net profit is the amount of money that remains after your business deduction is subtracted from your gross income. (Each business entity has its own rules for filing returns.)

Home-Based Business Tax Deductions. You may be entitled to claim some deductions for the part of your home that you use for your business. The IRS has never been fond of this opportunity, so be careful about claiming this type of deduction. Figure 12.4 is an outline of the current rules for such a deduction.

Figure 12.4: RULES FOR HOME TAX DEDUCTION

The general home tax deductions rules follow.

- The part of your home you deduct for tax purposes must be used regularly for your business.

- If you do use it regularly, it must be your principal place of business.

- If it is not your principal place of business, then it needs to be where you meet or deal with customers in the normal course of your business.

- If you run a day care facility, you can deduct the parts of your home you use for that enterprise.

- If you use a separate structure (like a garage or a barn), you can claim it as a deduction.

Self-Employment Tax. The federal self-employment tax is a term the IRS uses for the Social Security and Medicare taxes (FICA) that a self-employed person pays. This amount and other details of filing tax on your business depend on how your business is legally organized, the changing laws, and your own personal IRS annual filings. The FICA or the amounts that you contribute to Social Security and Medicare depend on what you are receiving as taxable income from your business. It may be beneficial for you to personally continue to make contributions to Social Security that provides you with retirement benefits; disability benefits (called SSI); survivor benefits for your spouse or dependents; and, health care insurance (Medicare).

Currently, the IRS considers all income as taxable or not taxable, depending upon your deductions. The deductions that are available for those who own their own business are as variable as the deductions available to all taxpayers. Depending on your business, you may even elect to pay taxes on a quarterly basis. (This and all other tax questions should be discussed with your tax accountant.)

Corporate Taxes: If you choose to operate as a type of corporation, there will be taxes on the corporation's net profits. In addition, as a corporate employee, your income will be taxed.

Employment Taxes. Your business will be required to process federal employment taxes only if you have employees. These taxes are: federal income tax withholding, Social Security and Medicare (FICA); and, federal unemployment (FUTA).

If you intend to hire employees, get IRS Publication 15, *The Employer's Tax Guide*. If you plan to hire agricultural employees, get the *Agricultural Employer's Tax Guide*. These publications explain the rules regarding your tax responsibilities as an employer. Understanding the IRS regulations can help you structure your business in both size and complexity.

Your state may have a law that requires you to participate in the state's unemployment tax program. Before you hire even one employee, check with your state regarding its legal requirements and you will also need to obtain a state unemployment tax number. If you do pay into a state unemployment tax program, you will get a credit from the federal government.

Excise Taxes. Excise taxes will apply if you intend to produce, sell, or import guns, tobacco, alcohol, or manufacture equipment for their production. There are also excise taxes on: substances that harm the environment; communications and air transportation; fuel; the first retail sale of heavy trucks, trailers, and tractors; and, luxury passenger vehicles.

State and Local Business Taxes. Most states have income taxes, even more have sales and use taxes. Each state will have its own special activities that it taxes. It will also have its forms and dates when these taxes are due. Part of your start-up work is to find out what your obligations will be. (See the Appendix for contact information for all Secretaries of State.) You will need to obtain your own state tax identification number, pay estimated taxes, and process withholding taxes.

You may also have to pay taxes to a city, town, or county. It might be called a tax or a fee. It may be labeled a permit. Your tax payment system needs to include all of these. Whatever your business activities are, check with the city and the county where you are conducting business to find out what their tax requirements.

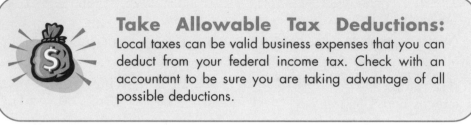

Take Allowable Tax Deductions: Local taxes can be valid business expenses that you can deduct from your federal income tax. Check with an accountant to be sure you are taking advantage of all possible deductions.

The Insurance Agent

The professional who is in the best position to help you define your insurance needs and shop for the best coverage is an insurance agent. An *independent agent* is one who sells for several insurance companies. There are also agents who sell insurance for only one insurance company. (If you already have home insurance from one company, you may be able to get a discount on business insurance from that same company.)

You have a right to expect an agent to understand your business, seek out the lowest possible premium rates, and give you good policy service. Other home-based business owners in your area refer you to possible insurance agents. In addition, your trade or professional association may sell or have a contract with a specific insurance company.

QUICK Tip

Preexisting Conditions: Try to find a policy that has no limitations on preexisting conditions. If you cannot find one, instruct your insurance agent that you are only interested in a policy with the maximum of a six-month exclusionary period.

Your Home Insurance Policy

One potential problem with running a business from your home can be the insurance coverage on your home. Depending upon your policy, you may not be covered for damage to the structure due to accidents caused by the business.

For example, if the home business is cookies and you purchase a large industrial stove, damages caused by the stove (fire, floor weakness, etc.) may not be covered by your home insurance policy.

Another example is if clients routinely come to your home to conduct their business. Your home insurance policy may not cover injuries caused by a client, or to a client, if those injuries are in conjunction with doing business.

Two ways to determine if your policy will protect you and your home business is to contact your insurance agent and to read your policy. You may need to add a rider to your home policy to protect you and those who enter your business. While this is yet another cost to doing business, the insurance cost is probably less than what a lawsuit might cost you later.

Health Care Insurance

Chances are that health care is the type of insurance you will use the most. If you are ill and unable to afford to get health care, you may be unable to continue with your business. This is especially true if you have employees.

The cost of this type of insurance for small business owners is very high. To help you solve this problem, check with your professional or trade association. If you are not a member, consider joining one, as these groups may have a way you can pool your dollars with others to purchase health-care insurance for you and your family.

QUICK Tip

Group Medical Insurance: Group insurance coverage has an excellent feature— it is usually issued without a medical examination or need for you to submit other medical evidence that could be used to exclude you.

Disability Insurance

Disability insurance may be important coverage for your home-based business. It is a way for you to be paid, even if you become ill and cannot work. These policies vary widely. A good insurance agent can find one tailored to your needs and budget. If you join a trade or professional association, it may offer you the opportunity to buy this coverage through them. Consider the costs of a disability insurance premium compared to the risk you take with the potential income loss to you and your family if your business loses you to a disability.

Coverage and Cost

When it comes to buying insurance, your top priority should be to buy what you need for your operation—but only what you need and can afford. Know how much money you would have to come up with if a financial loss materializes and you do not have insurance coverage.

Being Self-Insured

You may decide that you do not need or want to pay for insurance. As long as there are no legal impediments to being without insurance coverage, that is your choice to make. But know that it is a decision that will leave you self-insured for any financial losses that you may incur if a risk materializes.

If you choose to be self-insured, consider what your self-insured costs will be. For example, what will your health costs average year? If someone falls and is injured in your home, how much will it cost you to pay their medical bills and possible loss of income? If you are a professional and injure someone, how much will it cost in legal fees to defend yourself and pay any judgment against you? If your roof is damaged in a storm and falls on your work area, destroying some or all of your equipment and records, and preventing you to work until everything is replaced—how much money will you need to repair your roof and what amount of money will you need to survive on until your income resumes? Put those figures into your budget and determine how you will fund them. In other words, decide what it will cost if all the possible risks that could happen to your business actually occur.

Business Records

The first step to take to decide what business records you create and keep is to learn what the IRS and other governmental agencies require of your business. The complete set of requirements will depend upon your type of business—how the business is legally set-up (sole proprietorship, corporation, etc.), and if you have employees or use independent contractors.

Check your Secretary of State's website (see the Appendix) and see if it addresses the records you must retain in your state. Next, go to the IRS site at **www.irs.gov** to gather the information it provides for your type of business. Contact your local government units to determine if there are additional requirements.

Many of the records that you are required to keep are due to tax laws. This is truly a positive requirement and worth your effort, as these records will enable you to do two important things. First, it will help you take all the tax deductions to which you are allowed. Second, it will give you the proof needed to take the deductions should you be audited. Confer with your accountant or the attorney that assisted you in setting up your business for advice on what to keep.

By far the largest groups of records a business wants to have are those with a financial purpose. Although laws require many of these, keeping financial records provides you with a quick check to make sure that the business is doing well.

Many small businesses use accounting software to keep their financial records. There are several good software packages on the market. If that is how you intend to maintain your records, you will need to make time to do the data entry required. Remember to back-up all the data entered as frequently as possible. Minimally, data entry and back-ups should be done monthly, as a method to close out a month.

QUICK Tip

Consider All Your Options: For some home business owners, the price and the time required to use computer software is not practical. Many small businesses rely on a simple, basic paper income and expense system.

Create a Business Records System

As an owner of a home-based business, it is a good idea at the outset to create an uncomplicated, inexpensive, and effective method to keep track of your business expenses, income, and other business records. The system you set up should allow you to keep your personal and nonbusiness expenses and income separate from your business items. You want to have a record keeping system that is simple to use, easy to understand, reliable and accurate, kept in a consistent way, and designed to provide you with information on a timely basis.

An easy way to create a simple, but valuable method to track revenues and expenses, is to use a bunch of envelopes. At the beginning of the tax year, label each envelope with a category for a type of expense or business operation. Each time you get a receipt or other document, put it into the correct envelope, right away.

Alert!

File Your Information—Now: Do not let your filing pile up. While it may not seem like a high priority, you are more likely to keep accurate records when you regularly do your filing instead of waiting until a large pile amasses.

Instead of envelopes, you may choose to use files and folders to hold your papers. Several files can often be stored in one folder. Store your folders in a filing cabinet or filing box. Big box stores and office supply stores sell covered filing boxes in a variety of sizes. They are made of either cardboard or hard plastic.

Cash

If you accept cash, always give a receipt and retain a copy of each transaction via cash register tape, computer, or receipt book. Take cash deposits to your bank at least once a day. If less frequently, keep cash in a fireproof, spill proof, locked box. File each proof of deposit slip from your bank in its correct place as soon as you get back home.

1099 Forms

If you will receive 1099 forms from customers or clients (income you receive from each payee that is $600 or more) label an envelope "1099 forms." Each time you send an invoice, put a note in about the amount, client name, and date you received payment. At the end of each January, you will have an easy way to check off the 1099s as they come in and be sure that they are the correct amount. The IRS has a 1099 Matching Program. Be sure that the figure on the 1099 form you receive and report on your income tax match what the IRS has. Failure to have these numbers match can trigger an audit.

QUICK Tip

Record Keeping System: You can purchase elaborate record keeping systems at many office supply stores. The system you choose needs to be one you and your accountant can understand and use with ease. Also, check out the wide variety of software for this purpose.

SECTION V:

Manage Your Business Relationships

Chapter 13

Working with Customers

It is up to you, as a business owner, to develop good customer relationships by setting up policies before conflicts arise, treating each customer with respect, and putting the customer's needs before your own.

▶ **Developing Solid Customer Relations**
▶ **Customer Service Principles**
▶ **Customer Satisfaction Policy**
▶ **Customer Payment Policies**
▶ **Preparing Invoices**
▶ **Extending Credit**
▶ **Payment Problems**
▶ **Refund Policies**
▶ **Disputes**
▶ **Conflict Management Policy**
▶ **Contracts and Customer Relationships**

Developing Solid Customer Relations

Before you attract customers, you need to develop a policy that will guide your customer service activities. Whether you sell widgets or party planning services, your customers are crucial to your success. Without them, you will go out of business. Take time to decide what you want to see in your customer service policy.

Start yourself off right by understanding early on that good customer relations will help you to achieve your goals. You will discover that keeping your clients is as important as attracting new ones. Perhaps it is even more important. If you lose a customer because of a failed relationship, you are at risk to lose more. Remember, you are just starting out and the loss of even one customer can be a big blow to your income.

The same is true for relationships with your vendors, suppliers, distributors, subcontractors, and others. If you do not cultivate good working relationships with the people and businesses that you need to run your business, you may find yourself unable to service your customers properly.

Customer Service Principles

There are many things you can do to maintain good relationships. The best thing is to meet your customers' expectations. Use the principles in Figure 13.1 to let your customers know you appreciate their business.

Figure 13.1: PRINCIPLES OF GOOD CUSTOMER SERVICE

Follow these principles to help ensure good customer service.

- *Ask clients or customers what they want.* Survey potential consumers as you begin planning your business. Every so often you can survey or simply talk to customers once you are up and running.

- *Keep your promises.* Do not make promises that you cannot keep. Do not feel pressured into promising a customer something—just to get the business.

- *Be consistent.* Once you establish a level of performance that customers can expect; perform consistently with those expectations. Whether it is price, quality, delivery time, or terms, you cannot afford to meet expectations only some of the time. Customers will begin to choose another business with a reputation for consistency.

- *Be responsive.* Successful business people return phone calls and/or emails, promptly. Customers may have a problem that you could solve before it gets to the crisis level.

- *Be fair.* What is fair to some may not be fair to others. In some businesses, price is one of the most important aspects. At other times, what is fair is really a matter of being responsive to your customers.

- *Distinguish yourself from the competition.* Getting and keeping customers is all about making them want to do business with you, rather than your competitors. You cannot always know why a person chooses you over a competitor, but it does not hurt to offer a bit more than your competitors to make your business stand out. (It is not always about a better price.)

- *Thank your customers.* Simple words of gratitude play an important part in running your business. If yours is not a business where you meet customers face to face, then a note or email expressing your appreciation may be appropriate. If you have important customers that you want to keep, pick up the phone and call to simply say thanks.

Customer Satisfaction Policy

A *customer satisfaction policy* is how you respond when things go wrong. Most people do not expect perfection from a business. (Although, the degree to which precision matters differs according to the nature of the business.)

Mistakes happen. Things change. Unforeseen circumstances arise. What customers do not understand is a business that fails to take responsibility when mistakes happen or unfortunate things occur. They do not understand or forgive if the business owner keeps silent when unforeseen circumstances arise.

CASE STUDY: **The Half-Done Job**

You are hired to paint a house. Halfway into the job, you break your leg. If you had been the one hiring someone to paint your house and this happened, you certainly would expect an offer of several alternatives, such as the painter getting a colleague to finish the job, or being asked to wait but given a price break for the inconvenience.

This is a classic type of unforeseen circumstance. You would not want the painter to simply inform you that he or she plans to complete the job when his or her leg has healed. If you are the painter, your customer would not want to hear that either. Whether you are recommended to a neighbor or hired again in the future by this customer may depend upon how you handle the situation.

Customer Payment Policies

Getting payment for your product or service is very important. You have several options that enable your customers to pay for your product or service, such as cash, check, extending credit, or credit cards. This section describes payment options and notes some of the legal rules you need to follow regarding each.

Cash

Perhaps you will be in a business in which customers pay only in *cash*. To most people, cash is the word used for hard currency. But in the world of business and the IRS, cash means traveler's checks, cashier checks, certified checks, bank drafts, and money orders.

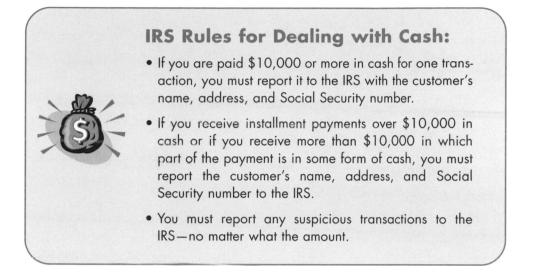

IRS Rules for Dealing with Cash:

- If you are paid $10,000 or more in cash for one transaction, you must report it to the IRS with the customer's name, address, and Social Security number.

- If you receive installment payments over $10,000 in cash or if you receive more than $10,000 in which part of the payment is in some form of cash, you must report the customer's name, address, and Social Security number to the IRS.

- You must report any suspicious transactions to the IRS—no matter what the amount.

Checks

You may determine that you will accept checks at the point of sale or service. If so, you need to understand that accepting checks is a risk that you do not have to take when you accept cash or credit cards. You may want or need to take that risk. If so, read the suggestions discussed in Figure 13.2 regarding a possible check acceptance policy.

Figure 13.2: TAKING CHECKS AS PAYMENT

Your policy for accepting checks can include such things as:

- getting identification, such as a driver's license or a state ID card;

- taking only checks issued by local banks;

- accepting checks for only the amount of the transaction or allow only a small amount of cash to be returned to the customer, such as $5 or $10;

- accepting no third-party checks, such as Social Security checks or paychecks;

- accepting no checks dated later than the date of the transaction;

- scanning each check you receive for the encoded bank and account information;

continued

- charging a fee for a check that bounces (your state may have a limit on the amount you can charge);

- using a stamp with the name of your business to endorse the check and deposit it on the day received; and,

- posting your check acceptance policy for customers to see. (If you do business in a community whose members speak another language, post it in that language, as well.)

Credit Cards

With credit cards, you will need to have a bank to process your payments and deposit them in your business account. You will pay bank handling fees of between 2% to 3% of a customer's bill for *Discover, MasterCard, Visa,* and other cards. *American Express* charges more. As you consider whether to allow your customers to use a credit card for purchasing your product or service, ask yourself the questions addressed in Figure 13.3.

Figure 13.3: SHOULD I ACCEPT CREDIT CARDS FOR PAYMENT?

Ask yourself the following to help determine if you should accept credit cards for payment.

- *What amount of fee do I want to pay for this service?* (Because the bank takes the collection risk, you need to know how much the service is worth to your business.)

- *Does the bank charge a service fee?* (Fees can range from an initial service fee, to an annual fee, to fees for the use of the credit card machine to handle your customer's card.)

- *What do I believe about my potential customers' credit card preferences?* (For instance, customers in remote rural areas with sparse tourist traffic may not want to use a credit card often enough to make it an affordable expense for your business.)

- *How quickly will I get paid?* (One to three days are the usual wait for the bank to deposit the funds in your account. Some credit card companies take longer.)

- *Is the certainty of getting my money worth the expense?* (You get your money even if the bank does not.)

Debit Cards

At this stage in their use, debit cards are rarely used by start-up, home-based businesses. This type of bill payment, however, is something you may choose to use for payment of some of your personal expenses. Banks are often eager to have you accept debit cards. There often is very little or no cost to the business owner for this service. This is an area that is still changing—check with your attorney before making a final decision.

Preparing Invoices

Instead of accepting payment immediately, you may discover that the custom in your type of business is sending invoices. You may prefer this technique to secure payment for your service or product. If you choose this method, be sure to prepare your bills regularly.

Regularly depends upon your business' activities and the billing custom in your type of business. Restaurants prepare their bills as you order. Other businesses send out bills monthly, quarterly, or even once a year. It truly is a formula that you can determine. It depends on the way things are done in the type of business you are in, what your customer expects, and what works for your situation.

> **Plan to Collect Payments:** Cash flow is critical to new, small businesses, so you need to plan your billing cycle appropriately. Collecting payments for your product or service should not come as an unplanned task for a new business owner.

Some businesses that work under contract will have the billing schedule described in the contract. If that is your business, be sure to prepare your bill with a regularity that makes sense to you. Whatever schedule preparation you choose, it needs to produce a bill that is an accurate description of the goods or services you provided. Figure 13.4 describes the issues that must be included in a billing statement for your business.

Figure 13.4: INFORMATION TO INCLUDE IN YOUR BILLING STATEMENT

In addition to your business name, mailing address, and phone number, your billing statement needs to include the following.

- *Payment due date.* (People need to know the deadline for paying a bill. You can specify a date or a time in relation to when you do your billing. If you indicate a payment due date, you must include the closing date of the billing period.)

- *Discount.* (If you want to encourage the payment to be made at the time the product or service is purchased, you can offer a discount of 5% or even 10%. You can also offer a discount if the payment is made earlier than the bill requires.)

- *Down payment.* (A down payment allows a business to get money for a product or service before delivery. This usually implies the business will do some work or incur some expenses before delivery.)

- *Installment payment details.* If you have worked it out with the customer before the purchase that it will be on an installment plan, be sure to number the statements and the balance remaining.

- *Finance charge.* (If you told the customer that late payments are subject to a finance charge, specify the percentage. If you do assess a finance charge, make sure it does not exceed your state's law.)

Billing Practices

The *Fair Credit Billing Act* describes your minimum obligations when a customer notifies you of an error. A customer has sixty days from when you mailed the bill to notify you of an error. You must respond within thirty days of when you first receive the complaint. You must investigate and tell the customer the results of the investigation within ninety days of the complaint. If you do not follow these steps exactly, you must give the customer a $50 credit. (Individual states have their own laws in this area. Often, these laws are tougher than the federal law.)

To promote goodwill, many businesses honor customers complaints, even if they notify the company after the sixty days has passed. If this is an issue in your kind of business, think about how you will factor the cost of this into your pricing practices.

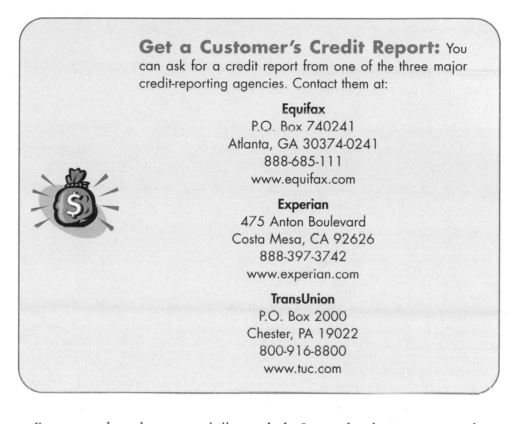

Get a Customer's Credit Report: You can ask for a credit report from one of the three major credit-reporting agencies. Contact them at:

Equifax
P.O. Box 740241
Atlanta, GA 30374-0241
888-685-111
www.equifax.com

Experian
475 Anton Boulevard
Costa Mesa, CA 92626
888-397-3742
www.experian.com

TransUnion
P.O. Box 2000
Chester, PA 19022
800-916-8800
www.tuc.com

Prepare and send out your bills regularly. It may be that you are paid on the date you deliver. In some types of business, statements are issued at the end of each quarter. Follow the custom in your type of business. People often expect that businesses do billing the way all of the others do. If you need to deviate, find a way to do it that preserves the customer relationship for the future. No matter what the custom is in your type of business, you may have a feeling about a certain customer that makes you want to send your bill right away. If this is the case, you should do so. Review the information in Figure 13.5 if you find yourself in a situation where you must actively collect payment.

QUICK Tip

Take the High Road with Your Customers: You may want to add a sentence to your bill that reads something like, *if you have any questions about your bill, please call.* This is a gracious gesture of goodwill that opens the door for the customer. He or she may complain. If so, you can work on taking care of it. This also gives you the opportunity to retain the business of the customer.

Figure 13.5: STEPS IN THE COLLECTION PROCESS

Take the following steps in your collection process.

- Always get your bills out on time.
- Send out a second notice.
- Send a third notice with a deadline.
- Call the customer if the deadline passes.
- Send an immediate follow-up letter to your call.
- Send a letter, return receipt requested, if you are unable to speak to the person on the phone.
- File a lawsuit in small claims court if the amount that is owed to you is small enough.
- If the amount is too big for the small claims court, sue in another court. (Of course, you will need to consider hiring a lawyer at this stage.)

Extending Credit

If you are going to extend credit, you need to get some credit information to assess the customer's credit worthiness and to get information to help with bill collection, if necessary. Ask your customer to complete a formal credit application. Make sure you get full name, phone number, address, employer, bank, and checking account number used for payment. You will also need in-depth information such as how long customers have lived at their current address, if they own or rent, the nearest relative not living with them, and the amount of annual income from all sources the customer wants used to calculate credit worthiness.

Extending credit has its pluses and minuses. If you decide to grant credit, there are several state and federal laws that regulate business owners and their dealings with customer credit. There are laws that protect the consumer and ones to protect you, the business owner. If you violate these laws, the financial penalties can be steep and you risk being sued. Lawsuits bring unwanted notoriety to a home business owner, so be sure that you have safe policies in place that you follow to extend credit and always follow the credit laws carefully.

Alert!

Understand the Credit Laws: Always follow the credit laws carefully. If you violate these laws, the financial penalties can be steep and you risk being sued.

Equal Credit Opportunity Act

You cannot discriminate against credit applicants because of race, color, religion, national origin, sex, marital status, or age. Doing so is a violation of the *Equal Credit Opportunity Act*. However, you do not have to accept someone who is not of legal age in your state to enter into a contract. Insufficient income, savings, or poor credit record are also valid reasons to reject an applicant.

Truth in Lending Act

According to the *Truth in Lending Act*, a business must tell each customer its precise credit terms concerning the amount of monthly finance charge, flat fee, annual interest rate, payment deadlines, total amount of all charges, and late payment fees or percentages. Under federal law, the consequences for violating disclosure requirements can be the imposition of substantial financial penalties. In addition, most states have laws that regulate credit disclosure practices. If the violations are deemed severe enough under your state law (laws vary from state to state), you could also face being fined by your state's authority. If the amount in question is large enough, it is possible that a customer could sue you for the damages they suffered as a result of your failing to disclose the full extent of your credit terms.

Payment Problems

If you run into nonpayment or partial payment problems, call or write the customer and then redeposit the check or reprocess the payment. If this does not work, have a collection agency handle the matter (if it will be cost effective). Next, file a lawsuit. If the amount is small, it may be best to go to the small claims court in your area. You will need to find out what the upper limits of a lawsuit can be when filed in this type of court in your state. Finally, call the police. They may want to prosecute. The key is speed in taking all of these steps. If you want your money, move quickly.

Alert!

Hire an Attorney: Be sure to know what state and federal laws require of you and the protection they give to consumers. It may be that you need to consult with a small business lawyer to help you put together a policy that stays within all legal mandates of collection payments.

Each state has its own laws that must be followed regarding collecting payments. Learn what they are—do research on your own if you think that collecting payment will put you at legal risk. Figure 13.6 lists activities that you should avoid when bill collecting becomes necessary.

Figure 13.6: **AVOID THE FOLLOWING BILL COLLECTING TACTICS**

The following bill collecting tactics should be avoided.

• Threaten violence

• Pretend to be a police officer

• Pretend to be from the government

• Threaten to a call an employer

• Harass the debtor or the debtor's family

• Pretend to be a lawyer

• Publish the debt and the name of the debtor on the Internet, newspaper, or elsewhere

• Call before or after the hours allowed for debt collection telephone calls

• Tell the customer's friends, associates, neighbors or colleagues

---

QUICK Tip

Being Right May Not Always Be in Your Best Interest: Even if you are right, you may want to drop the matter because of customer relations or your costs to pursue the customer. These are valid business reasons that might outweigh a difficult collection decision.

Refund Policies

You will encounter a time when a customer wants a refund. Be prepared to meet this problem with a policy that you and your employees can implement immediately—without fuss and with much grace. Many businesses keep it simple. They print on the receipt that the item can be returned within a certain number of days, weeks, or months and that the original receipt must accompany the item. Many businesses routinely issue gift card receipts with the charge receipt to enable anyone to return an item without fuss.

> **QUICK Tip**
>
> Post Your Return Policy: Choose a return policy you can work with consistently. Keep track of what the competition does and meet or beat it. Make your policy one with which you feel comfortable. Communicate it in some way to your customers and to all of your employees.

Consistent refund policies can endear you to customers. They can earn you the reputation of a business that is good to do business with. This reputation helps you to keep customers satisfied and willing to recommend to others that they do business with you. If you discover that people in your community abuse your return policy, you can always revise it to suit your situation.

Disputes

No matter how careful you are there may come a time when a legitimate dispute between your customer and yourself arises. The following are some terms you may hear in a legal dispute.

Mediation

Mediation is a process for resolving disputes. It is simply a negotiation that is structured and facilitated by a mediator. The parties who are involved choose the mediator. However, it is important in the business world to have someone who is not involved in the dispute. Parties need to be able to trust that what they tell the mediator will be kept confidential until they are ready to tell the other side. If you find yourself in a business dispute, review the benefits of mediation discussed in Figure 13.7.

Figure 13.7: BENEFITS OF MEDIATION

In addition to being an affordable and cost efficient technique, mediation has several other desirable qualities for home-based businesses.

- *It is private.* There is no public record made during mediation. The parties agree to keep everything confidential and the laws of most states uphold that benefit.

- *Relationships are preserved.* Partnerships, vendors, suppliers, customers, and other relationships that are important to your business can be preserved and strengthened through the use of mediation.

- *The parties maintain control.* In mediation, the parties make the decisions. No judge, no jury, no arbitrator decides the matter.

- *Win/Win.* You might not fully like what you agree to, but you should feel that it is fair and that the process was fair. In a typical mediation, the other side will feel the same way. Each of you will give value to the other. You will gain closure and certainty. There are no losers in mediation.

Just because you really want to resolve the dispute with the help of a mediator does not mean the other party is so motivated. Business mediations are voluntary. No one has to agree to the terms of a mediated agreement. Not everyone has what it takes to participate in mediation.

QUICK Tip

Mediation and Success: Mediation is popular because it is so highly effective— 85% of all disputes that are mediated are resolved. This high rate of resolution is because the disputing parties can keep control of the process; they enter into it voluntarily; and, they can create solutions that are unavailable in a court of law.

Alert!

Mediation for Money: Never choose a mediator who offers to work for a percentage of the outcome. This is unethical under most mediator codes of ethics.

Arbitration

When mediation does not result in an agreement, the next step in the dispute resolution process is often *arbitration*. This process is almost like a court trial. There is someone called an arbitrator, who makes a decision like a judge or jury would. There can be lots of very expensive paperwork and preparation. Businesses cannot keep control of the outcome.

There are some differences between arbitration and litigation. For one, unlike a trial, the arbitration process is private. There is not usually a court reporter. The courtroom rules of evidence do not apply. This means the parties have a better opportunity to tell their side.

It is usually less expensive. It does not take as long from the time you ask to arbitrate until the arbitrator's award is handed down. The arbitrator's decision is final. There is very rarely a right of appeal to a higher court.

Litigation

The last step in resolving disputes is to file a lawsuit. Even if you win—you lose. It is expensive, time consuming, and emotionally draining. The energy you need to devote to a lawsuit saps the vigor you need to devote to your business. It diverts your attention, possibly for years, until your trial is scheduled and completed.

Litigation as a way to resolve a dispute makes sense only if there is a unique issue of law at stake. However, when there is an issue of law to be decided, your case may very well be appealed making the time until your case is finally over, even more years away.

Conflict Management Policy

A small business should have a conflict management policy that is ethical, efficient, and cost effective. Your strategies can include dispute prevention, identification, and resolution. The benefits of such a policy should include: customer goodwill and satisfaction; vendor and supplier loyalty; and, a decrease in exposure to lawsuits, less legal fees, and a decrease in litigation costs.

CASE STUDY: Party Dresses and Mom

Lois makes children's clothes for special and social events. Each garment is a one-of-a-kind, hand-designed creation. Ida was a wealthy woman that was very fussy about how she dressed her children. She contacted Lois about creating two formal dresses for the coming out party of her twin daughters. During the fifteen fittings, Ida continued to change her mind about the dresses. At two of the fittings, the girls and Ida got into a heated argument about how the dresses would look. On the date of the pick up, Ida announced that the finished products were not to her standards and she refused to pay for the dresses.

At that point, Lois had several hundred dollars of material in the dresses, plus many hours of sewing. Lois had a Conflict Management Policy that basically put customer satisfaction over her monetary loss. While Lois was hurt and angry at the treatment from Ida, she did not yell or threaten to sue her. Lois calmly explained that she had a lot invested in the dresses, but if they were not up to Ida's standards, she would fix them so they were.

Because Lois did not lose her temper, she and Ida were able to decide calmly what needed to be done to make the dresses perfect. Lois not only saved the sale, but her professional demeanor and decision to put the customer first resulted in many referrals from Ida for years to come.

Contracts and Customer Relationships

A *contract* is an agreement between two parties. There are two essential elements in a contract—the give and the get. In a contract, each party gets something and each party gives something. When you buy a service or a product from a vendor, what you get is that business' service or product. What you give to the vendor is the price the vendor sells it to you for. Having a well-written contract can clearly spell out the expectations of both sides and lead to less frustrations if a problem arises. Review the information in Figure 13.8 as you begin to develop a customer contract.

Figure 13.8: CUSTOMER CONTRACT TERMS

The following are mandatory items that must be in your contracts with customers.

- Price terms
- Number of units to be delivered
- Estimated hours and/or type of service and description of anticipated extent of service
- Date of delivery of product or service
- Your name and the names of anyone else in the deal
- Your signature and the signatures of all involved in the deal
- The date of each signature

It does not have to be an extremely formal document. You can use a piece of your letterhead. You can use a pad of paper that has your business name, address, and phone number on it. These are only the minimum terms you need to negotiate and put in a contract. Many deals are likely to require more contract terms.

Try as you might to make a contract cover every detail, sometimes you will meet a situation that is not covered. When that happens, it is best to keep in mind the principles of good customer relations. To be sure that all your contract terms comply with the law, you may want to ask your attorney to draft several generic contracts for your business.

CASE STUDY: Why Terms of a Contract Are So Important

Ted's home-based business is assembling and selling a small, portable wading pool filtration system made to the specifications of the customer. His parts come from many different suppliers across the country and his customers are all over the world. Ted has a great website for his business that allows customers to design their filtration system, place an order, and send in a signed contract with a deposit.

Ted must decide how to handle the issue of shipping costs. If the contract is not clear on who pays shipping costs, Ted may end up paying for customs delays and off loading in some countries. In addition, contracts that are vague annoy customers because the customers do not understand the real total cost.

On one hand Ted does not want to pay the entire shipping cost, but on the other hand, it may cost less in the long run to cover those shipping costs, if it keeps customers happy and returning to buy more. Ted decided to pay for the cheapest form of delivery in the United States; allow the customer to pay for a speedier delivery; and, to pay a flat limit on the shipping costs out of the country.

Contract disputes can be of special concern for new businesses. You may want to do what many small businesses are doing these days—negotiate into every contract a clause that addresses how disputes will get resolved.

Chapter 14

Working with Vendors

Many home-based businesses will need to obtain supplies or equipment from other businesses or vendors. The quality of these items can be especially important when the vendor products are a major component in what you provide.

▸ **Negotiation Guidelines**
▸ **Negotiating Contracts with Vendors**

Negotiation Guidelines

Following the negotiation guidelines in Figure 14.1 will give you confidence, (even if you currently think you are a horrid negotiator). If you really learn how to use them, you and your business will benefit. Use them to get and keep clients or customers. Use them to get the terms you want with backers or suppliers. Use them to enhance employee relations.

Figure 14.1: TWELVE POINTS TO EFFECTIVE NEGOTIATION

Use these twelve points for effective negotiations.

1. Be Prepared. Negotiating from a position of strength and knowledge is the best place to be when negotiating with others to get exactly what it is that you want.

2. Goals. Make a written list of what you want to achieve—then prioritize it.

3. Issues. Make a written list that includes everything that relates to your goals. If you are buying a computer, some issues might be software capacity, affordability, and service.

4. Options. Know going in what your options are. It will help you achieve flexibility.

5. Best Choice. Be prepared to choose from among the best options so your start-up plans will not be held up any longer than necessary by not getting your first choice.

6. Bottom Line. Identify the point beyond which you will not go—this is your bottom line. This is the serious point in the negotiations where you decide that either you get it or you walk away.

7. Initial Position. This is your starting point in the negotiation process. Do not make it unrealistic or you will not be taken seriously.

8. Fall-Back Position. Your fall-back position is somewhere above your bottom line and below your initial position.

9. Your Needs. Know what you need, not merely what you want. This will allow you to think outside the box.

10. Other Person's Shoes. Once you prepare for each of the previous nine points, do the same kind of preparation as if you were the person across the table. You will not get it perfect, but you will come close enough to even the playing field for yourself.

continued

11. Win/Win. This is an outcome and an attitude. You want to win, but not at the expense of the other person losing. People who feel good about negotiating with you will want to do business with you.

12. Good Faith. Negotiating in good faith is important for your reputation and your business. This encompasses honesty, integrity, and decency.

Negotiating Contracts with Vendors

When you are just starting out, you may need equipment and supplies. (See Chapter 3 for some of the equipment and supplies a new, home-based business may need.) Your financial resources are greatly limited and so you need to compensate by doing three things.

1. Maximize your financial resources to achieve your goals.
2. Research what you want to acquire and your potential vendors.
3. Negotiate from a position of strength to get what you need for your business.

The same is true when you seek to put your product into the marketplace. You may choose to distribute your product directly to the consumer through your own shop or on the Internet. If you need to find outlets, then you will need to negotiate with vendors for distribution channels. You will need to get the best deals you can, so you can have your product delivered to customers. You want those deals to give your new business a chance to compete with companies that are already in (what may be) a crowded marketplace.

Maximize Your Financial Resources

If you can afford to, it is always a good to pay cash. You usually avoid interest and penalties if you can use cash. If you cannot use cash, look for opportunities like finance plans and leases.

Finance Plan. A *finance plan* is a contract that has all the consequences of a legal agreement. Some manufacturers and dealers are willing to enter into this type of a contract with you in order to finance some or all of the cost of equipment. They usually let you pay each month over a set period of time—like one to five years. They usually charge interest. Some of these contracts let you own it subject to a mortgage, so you have to pay it off to really own it. Some will not let you own the title to the equipment until you pay for it in full.

These arrangements have two things for which to watch out. First, the equipment could have a life-use shorter than the length of the finance plan. You could wind up paying for it after the equipment becomes useless. Second, it is unlikely you will be allowed to sell or trade it during the time you are still paying for it.

Leasing Plan. *Leasing* equipment may be another option for your business. You can find sources for leasing everywhere you find sources for purchasing. Today you can lease just about anything, including desk chairs and computers. With electronic equipment in particular, one advantage to leasing may be the ability to easily exchange outdated equipment as new technology emerges. Figure 14.2 reviews some of the terms you must be aware of before you enter into a lease agreement.

Figure 14.2: LEASE TERMS YOU SHOULD KNOW

Know the answer to these lease questions *before* you lease.

- *Is it an open-ended lease?* In an open-ended lease, you have to make periodic payments throughout the life of the lease. The risk in this type of arrangement is that if the equipment is worth less than what the lease contract says it should be worth, then you have to pay the difference. It is called a wear-and-tear clause. (In open-ended leases, you bear the risk and it could be substantial.)

- *Is it a close-ended lease?* This type of contract is likely to be a better deal for most small businesses. This type of contract allows you to turn in the equipment at the end of the lease with no risk that you will have to pay any additional money.

- *Is there a balloon payment at the end of the lease?* You may be able to obtain a lease with monthly payments of a small, affordable amount. However, at the end of the lease term, you may have a large payment due. To make this work for your business, you have to plan ahead. You have to plan as far ahead as the number of months or years that you have before the lease is up and the balloon payment is due.

Assess Your Financial Position

As you contemplate whether to acquire equipment through a finance plan, a lease, or cash, evaluate your situation by asking yourself the questions in Figure 14.3.

Figure 14.3: DETERMINE YOUR OPTIONS FOR PAYMENT

Ask yourself the following questions to help determine the best payment option for you.

- What is the least expensive piece of relevant equipment that I can find?
- Will my cash flow cover payments, even if I have a seasonal operation?
- How much is the down payment?
- What is the length of the contract?
- What is the amount of the monthly payment?
- Will there be a balloon payment due? If so, when and how much?
- Is there a warranty? If so, what does it cover and what does it cost?
- What is the total cost of the lease or finance plan, including finance charges, down payment, balloon or other final payment, and warranty or extended service contract?
- Is maintenance included in a lease? If not, what are the maintenance costs?
- Are insurance costs covered in the lease? If not, what are the insurance costs?
- What are the tax consequences of your choice?

As a new business owner, you may find it difficult to lease because your business has no credit history. Depending on the size and nature of your business, leasing in your own name may be an option. This, of course, means you need to have a positive, personal credit history.

Research Potential Vendors

Whether you want your local supermarket, a bookstore, or some other type of appropriate business to sell your product, you will have to treat these vendors as a problem to solve. Figure 14.4 identifies detailed research steps you can take to evaluate a vendor.

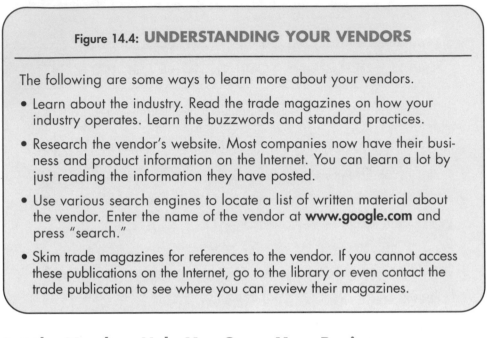

Figure 14.4: UNDERSTANDING YOUR VENDORS

The following are some ways to learn more about your vendors.

- Learn about the industry. Read the trade magazines on how your industry operates. Learn the buzzwords and standard practices.

- Research the vendor's website. Most companies now have their business and product information on the Internet. You can learn a lot by just reading the information they have posted.

- Use various search engines to locate a list of written material about the vendor. Enter the name of the vendor at **www.google.com** and press "search."

- Skim trade magazines for references to the vendor. If you cannot access these publications on the Internet, go to the library or even contact the trade publication to see where you can review their magazines.

Let the Vendors Help You Grow Your Business

If you are looking to make an impression on a vendor, nothing is better than to let them know you were interested enough to do some research on them.

When doing research look for positive things, like bringing out a new product or the winning of an award. Look for articles written by the owners of this company, as this may explain their business philosophy.

Ask questions. Yes, that makes you look like you don't know something, but it also says you care about your work. Most people are happy to answer a legitimate question about how things are done. Many of us are even flattered that we are thought of as an expert. If you do not know what a vendor's standard policy is—ask. If you are confused as to why something is done in a certain way—ask.

Ask your vendor how he or she could help you improve your business. Many times an experienced vendor can help you expand your product or change it in a way that will attract more customers. There is always a chance that a vendor may come up with an idea that will make your home-based business the *next great business*. (Of course, that would also make you the vendor's lifelong customer.)

Chapter

Working with Employees

You may start your home business with one worker—you. While you may be able to do it all at first, at some time you may decide to hire employees.

- ▶ **Choose the Correct Employment Category**
- ▶ **Write a Job Description**
- ▶ **Interview Process**
- ▶ **Check References**
- ▶ **The Decision Process**
- ▶ **Employment Compensation**
- ▶ **Employer Tax Responsibilities**

Choose the Correct Employment Category

In the majority of situations, it will make little difference as to the category an employee falls as few home based businesses have a large number of employees. However, a short explanation of each category follows.

Employee

Legally, an *employee* is someone who is controlled by another to do a certain task for compensation. While an employee is working for his or her employer, that employee is considered an agent of the employer or, in other words, is legally allowed to act for the employer. The employer is obligated to take the required taxes from an employee's paycheck.

> **EXAMPLE:** If part of an employee's duties is to deliver goods and that employee gets into an auto accident, the employer can be held responsible because the employee was acting for the employer. On the other hand, if the employee, in the course of his delivery, takes a side trip on his own and without permission, and then is in an auto accident, the employer will probably not be held liable. If you have employees and you send them to deliver or pick up items, talk to your insurance agent to make sure that these types of auto trips are covered.

Temporary Employee

There are two types of temporary employees: one who is working shorter hours or for a limited period of time for the employer, and the other is an employee of a temporary agency assigned to work for the employer. For the first type of temporary employee, all the legal implications of an employee are in effect.

When the temporary employee is acquired through an agency, the agency pays the employee's salary and takes the appropriate tax deductions from the employee's paycheck. The agency bills the employer for the hours the employee worked. Hiring and employee from a temporary agency eliminates the need for the employer to deal with paying taxes for employees, but it can be more expensive, as salaries are usually higher.

Independent Contractor

An independent contractor is an employee who takes care of his or her own taxes, Social Security deductions, Medicare deductions, and health care benefits. The employer is required to produce a 1099 form at the end of the year that lists all the money paid to the independent contractor. A copy of the 1099 is sent to the contractor and to the IRS. The contractor will then pay taxes on that amount. Hiring independent contractors eliminates the need for the employer to deal with paying taxes for employees.

Write a Job Description

The search for the right person starts with the creation of a job description. You want a person that has particular skills and abilities that add to your own. The first step to take is to decide what you want the worker to do. Use Figure 15.1 to gather information you can use to develop a job description.

Figure 15.1: DEVELOP A JOB DESCRIPTION

Determine the following information:

- exact needs that you have;
- specific duties, responsibilities, and authority you want in the new position;
- goals and objectives of the position;
- knowledge and skills required for the work;
- education and experience necessary to make the position valuable to you;
- physical requirements;
- special problems or hazards; and,
- any background checks that will be done.

You will not get the job description perfect, but you will come close. You may discover that after someone fills the position, both of you will be able to see what should be added, subtracted, or changed.

One of the big advantages to crafting a job description is that it can help you figure out if you want an employee, a temporary staff member, an independent contractor, or if you want to subcontract the work. It can also help you assess whether a collaborator is more appropriate for your business.

Job descriptions have another advantage. They help make it crystal clear to an employee what his or her duties and responsibilities are. Job descriptions also make your supervisory duties easier because you will have a clear idea of what you want your employee doing.

QUICK Tip

How to Develop a Classified Ad:
- Write the job description
- Analyze the publication for want-ad examples
- Review your ad to make sure it conforms to the law
- Contact the publication—one of its ad specialists may be able to help you make your ad stand out or reword it for better attention

Interview Process

The way to pick good résumés to pursue is to choose those that most closely match the skills, abilities, experience, training, or education that you want for your business and have included in your job description for the position. Once the phone calls and résumés come in, choose the top five people who most closely meet your requirements to interview. Five will give you a reasonable sampling of the people that are interested in your ad. If you are on your own and you decide to let people call you, keep the calls short. They may want to engage in an interview process over the phone, but your sole focus should be to screen them. You will want to be well-prepared and organized to meet and evaluate each interviewee. (Many small business owners have used the tips in Figure 15.2 to ensure a successful interview.)

Figure 15.2: FOCAL POINTS OF THE INTERVIEW PROCESS

Follow these points to learn as much as you can during an interview.

- *Be prepared.* Know the questions you want to ask. Write them down ahead of time on a master sheet or template. Photocopy a fresh one for each interview and take notes on that paper.

- Put together the questions that will get you the information you need to know about each person's:

  - experience;

  - professional goals;

  - knowledge; and,

  - skills that will make them a good addition to your new venture.

Interview Questions and the Law

Create a checklist of questions that meet not only the federal legal standards, but also ones that meet your state's standards. Review the information listed in Figure 15.3 in order to avoid potential legal problems during the interview process. Use your written checklist of standards and questions as your master sheet. Copy it and use it at each interview.

Focus your interview questions around those listed in Figure 15.4. At the end of the interview, put your signature on it and the time and date of the interview. Make up a new master sheet for each type of job. Stick to the questions on that sheet.

When you hire an applicant, put that interview sheet into the employee's file. Keep the interview sheets of those you don't hire in a separate file. (If you reject someone, you will have that person's interview questions available—just in case.)

Figure 15.3: DO NOT ASK QUESTIONS CONCERNING THE FOLLOWING TOPICS

The following topics can have legal ramifications that can get you into trouble.

- Religion or creed. (If your concern is about work schedule, inform each applicant through the ad and in the job description about the hours you need. In the interview, confirm that each applicant will be available for the time periods you need.)

- Age. (Inform applicants through the ad and job description the physical requirements of the job. Do not ask—"What year did you graduate from high school?", "Where did you go to college?", or "How old are you?" If the candidate is obviously older than you, do not ask something like—"How do you feel about taking orders from someone younger than you?")

- Marital status. (Do not ask if a person is married, living with someone, or is divorced. It can be considered discrimination to base hiring or firing on these facts.)

- Background. (Avoid asking about an arrest record. If this issue is important to you, a legal background check will reveal convictions in the last five years.)

- Sex or sexual orientation. (Do not ask a person what sex he or she is unless it is somehow an important part of the job, such setting up living in same-sex dormitories. Do not ask about sexual orientation or opinions on things such as *gay marriage*. It can be considered discrimination to base hiring or firing on a person's sexual orientation.)

- Color or national origin. (Do not ask a person what color or national origin they consider themselves. This is none of an employer's business and can constitute discrimination.)

- Disabilities. (Do not ask about physical impairments and illnesses that you feel might prevent an applicant from performing the job.)

- Date and type of military discharge. (Do not ask about military service. Even though as an employer you may want to know if a person can be called to active duty, not hiring or firing a person because of military service is discriminatory and illegal under several state and federal laws. Do not ask about the type of discharge a person got from the military. Unless you are the military, this information is not part of any job.)

- Children. (Do not ask if the person has children, if the person has day care planned, or if the person intends to be absent when a child is ill. If you provide day care services for your employee's children, offer it to everyone—even those who do not talk about children.)

- Pregnancy. (Never ask a woman if she can conceive or if she intends to have children. This is the #1 mistake employers make. Because only a woman can be pregnant, this type of question is considered blatant sex discrimination.)

- Weight and height. (If the job includes lifting 100-pound bags of grain throughout each eight-hour shift, put that into the job description.)

If you are concerned about what questions to avoid in your state and local community, you may want to have your attorney review them.

Figure 15.4: FOCUS YOUR INTERVIEW QUESTIONS

The following five points will help you to focus your interview questions. The answers will give you the information you need in order to make an educated decision.

1. Is the applicant qualified (experience, skills, knowledge, and ability) for the job you are offering?

2. Is the person willing to do the work you need done when you want it done?

3. Does the person have a personality you can work with?

4. Does the person have the credentials and experience he or she claims to have?

5. Is the applicant honest, reliable, and trustworthy?

Check References

Ask for references and check them. Many companies will only give you the dates people worked for them. (One of the most common exaggerations on resumes is where people worked and for how long.)

Do not limit your calls to those named by an applicant. Expand your reference gathering opportunities by asking each person you contact for three names of other people who know the applicant. Then contact each one and ask them for other names. Keep up this process until you are satisfied that you have acquired solid information about the applicant's knowledge, skills, abilities, and experience relevant to the position you are seeking to fill.

The Decision Process

Before you make your final decision, talk with all of the applicants you have decided to interview. Tell each one that you will be making a decision soon and will let them know your decision. You are in control of when you want someone to start, but understand that if you are slow to decide, your number one choice may not wait.

Once you make your decision, contact that person and offer the job. Figure 15.5 can provide you with legal suggestions for making an offer of employment. Whether that person says yes or no determines what you do next. If that person rejects your offer, select from the others you interviewed. You can always start the process over again. (This time you may want to put in your ad that the position has been reopened or you can say that you are still hiring.)

> ### Figure 15.5: SUGGESTION WHEN MAKING A JOB OFFER
>
> Use the following suggestion when making a job offer.
>
> - Do not say or write such things as—"We look forward to a long and rewarding experience with you in our business." (This gives the impression that this employee cannot and will not be fired at your discretion.)
>
> - Describe the terms and conditions of employment in writing. (Include a statement that these terms replace any oral promises made by anyone. Sign, date, and give a copy to the employee. Keep a copy in your files and put a copy in that person's personnel file.)
>
> - To help ensure that the employment relationship is at will (meaning you can terminate it at anytime for any legal reason), quote compensation frequency by payment. (Say that compensation is X dollars per week not in Y dollars per year. This helps show you are not offering some sort of yearly employment contract. You can then add that this is a yearly rate of Y dollars.)

Follow Government Regulations

Immediately after making an offer, check with the applicant for his or her immigration status. (No business is too small to avoid this federal law.) Get Form I-9, *Employment Eligibility Verification*, online at **www.uscis.gov** (U.S. Citizenship and Immigration Services). Follow the instructions for accurate completion.

With the passage in 1996 of the federal *Personal Responsibility Work Opportunity Reconciliation Act* (also known as the *Welfare Reform Act*), the government began to require the reporting of information on newly-hired employees. This Act seeks to identify and locate parents with delinquent child support payments through the New Hire Registry. The employer has twenty days to report the following information to the designated state agency.

- Employee
  Name, Address, and Social Security number
- Employer
  Name, Address, and EIN of the employer

QUICK Tip

New Hire Registry: If you need further information regarding the New Hire Registry, visit the website of the Office of Child Support Enforcement (under the Administration for Children and Families) at **www.acf.hhs.gov**.

Professional Etiquette

When a person accepts your position, send letters to the remaining interviewed applicants saying that the position has been filled and thanking them for their interest. It is a good idea to send this type of goodwill letter. You never can tell if you may want to recruit one of these people again. Even if not, it is a goodwill gesture that may serve your business' reputation in your community.

Employment Compensation

There are many legal and financial issues related to having employees. These include such items as the following.

- Minimum wage. (The federal *Fair Labor Standards Act* and some state laws regulate this matter.)
- Tips. (In many states, employers must pay a minimum wage to employees who earn tips.)
- Deductions from wages. (Federal and some state laws limit what an employer may deduct from wages.) Some items that many laws allow include:
  - union dues;
  - insurance—group accident and health, hospitalization;
  - contributions to credit unions, community chest fund, local arts council, local science council, and political action committees; and,
  - contributions to an employee stock purchase plan or savings plan.

Employer Tax Responsibilities

If you have employees, your business will be required to handle federal income tax withholding, Social Security, and Medicare (FICA), and federal unemployment (FUTA). IRS Publication 15, *The Employer's Tax Guide* is the authority on employee taxes. Because the tax laws change every year, make sure you get a current copy of this publication. You can go to **www.irs.gov** for more information.

QUICK Tip

Tax Software: You can install and use one of several brands of software to help you organize your tax collection responsibilities. Review the current software programs at your local computer store.

Employment Records

If you choose to have employees, you will have employee records that you must keep. The information that laws require you to keep current includes each employee's:

- name;
- address;
- occupation;
- Social Security number;
- hourly rate of pay;
- number of hours worked each pay period;
- amount of gross pay earned during each pay period;
- a list of deductions made from each paycheck;
- the net amount of pay in each pay period (after all deductions); and,
- the date each pay period ends.

Conclusion

One of our goals in writing this book was to validate and make use of our business experiences, both positive and negative. As sole proprietors, we have often found ourselves learning very valuable business lessons, but having no one to share the hard-earned knowledge with. This book is our attempt to share these experiences with you so that you may never be forced to learn the hard way.

We thank you for trusting in our assistance. We hope that we have provided a useful tool for you to fulfill your dream of having a home-based business. We wish you tons of success and prosperity for the future and leave you with one of our favorite quotes.

"Go confidently into the direction of your dreams!
Live the life you always imagined."
— Henry David Thoreau (1817-1862)

Glossary

A

account. A record of a business transaction.

account balance. The difference between the debit and the credit sides of an account.

accounting method. System for a business to keep financial information and report it to the proper taxing body.

accounts receivable. A record of the total number of sales made through the extension of credit.

accrual method. Method of keeping accounts that shows expenses incurred and income earned for a given period of time, even if these expenses or income have not actually been paid or received in that period.

arbitration. Presenting the details of a dispute to an impartial third party or panel to settle the dispute. Arbitration can be made mandatory by certain courts.

assumed name. An alias. Using another name.

B

bait and switch. Illegal practice of advertising a product or service at one price to get customers interested in buying and then trying to sell it to them at a higher price.

barter. To exchange services or property with someone who has property or services you need.

billing statement. Document listing what is owed.

bottom line. A summary that indicates what something really costs or can indicate profits after expenses are deducted.

budget. An organizations' estimated resources and expenses for a specific period of time.

business plan. A way to track strategies, sales projections, and key personnel. Also, a road map for marketing activities, mission implementation, goals, raising and spending business income, and financing administration needs. (Often called an operations plan.)

business structure. A term for how your business is organized. Can also refer to an organizational chart of who does what job.

buying on time. Making installment payments on an item, instead of paying the total amount all at once.

C

C corporation. A way of organizing a business, which has certain rules set up by each state.

cash flow. Amount of and frequency with which a business receives payments.

cash method. Method of keeping accounts by recording income and expenses only when they are paid out or received.

capital. Money or resources that are available for investment in a business.

collaborator. Colleague or teammate.

collateral. Property that is pledged as security against a debt.

competition. The action of two or more commercial interests to obtain the same business from third parties.

competitive research. Research done to obtain an edge on competitors.

conflict management policy. A predetermined business policy for handling disputes with customers, vendors, and others in running the business.

consignment store. Store that sells goods made by others. The purchase price includes a percentage kept by the store.

contract. A legal agreement between at least two parties.

corporation. A specific way a business can be organized. Each state determines its own rules regarding corporations.

credit rating. A numerical value determined by a person's or a corporation's history in paying bills.

D

deductions. An amount subtracted from gross income when calculating adjusted gross income.

depreciation. Process that allows a business to spread out a deduction over several years. Depreciation can only be used for certain items, such as equipment and furniture.

discount. An allowance or deduction made from a gross sum.

doing business as (d/b/a). When a business uses a name other than the name of the owner.

E

employer identification number (EIN). The taxpayer identification number a business will use for all the documents and tax returns that a business files with the IRS. A business must obtain it if it has one or more employees.

entrepreneur. Someone who organizes a venture and accepts the risks in hopes of profit.

Equal Credit Opportunity Act. Law enacted that prohibits a creditor from discriminating against any credit applicant on the basis of race, sex, color, religion, national origin, or marital status.

estimated taxes. Quarterly taxes for businesses that expect to owe taxes of $1,000 or more.

excise tax. Additional tax imposed on the performance of an act, the engaging in an occupation, or the enjoyment of a privilege. Common term for any license fee or any tax, except income tax.

F

Fair Credit Billing Act. Law enacted to facilitate settlement of billing error disputes and to make credit card companies more responsible for the goods purchased by the cardholder.

Federal Trade Commission. Governmental body that enforces laws on price-fixing, false advertising, trade restraints, and other matters of commerce.

fictitious name. A name used by a business that is not its personal, legal name.

finance plan. Written steps and goals for financing a business.

fiscal year. The dates a business's accounting year begins and ends. It is often the same as the calendar year, but a business can choose any one-year cycle of dates that best suits it.

franchise. Purchase of a right to run an existing business that is part of a well-known chain of businesses. It usually includes the use of the business's name, marketing, policies, and other objects the public associates with this business.

G

general partnership. A business that is owned by two or more persons.

goal. The actions taken to achieve a business purpose.

H

home equity. The amount of ownership that a person has paid into his or her home. Usually expressed as how much mortgage principal has been paid.

homeowners association. A legal organization that manages certain real estate.

I

identity theft. Taking on another person's persona for illegal purposes. Usually includes the use of Social Security numbers, credit card information, and other confidential details.

image. The impression the public has of a business's product, service, and business.

income-based budgeting. Money spent each year on expenses that does not exceed annual income.

independent contractor. An employee who pays his or her own taxes and benefits.

intellectual property. The legal term that refers to the assets created by mental exertions, such patents, copyrights, and trademarks.

inventory. The portion of a financial statement that reflects the value of a business' raw materials, works-in-progress, and finished products.

Internal Revenue Service (IRS). Branch of the U.S. Treasury Department responsible for administering the Internal Revenue Code and providing taxpayer education.

L

legal form. This is the structure of the business in the eyes of the law. It could be a corporation, partnership, or sole proprietorship.

liability. Broad legal term that is commonly used to mean a legal responsibility.

license. A state or federal approval given to a business or person who has fulfilled certain criteria such as education or testing.

limited liability company. A legal business organization that protects the owners of the business similar to those who own large corporations.

limited liability partnership. A legal business organization term that is used in some states. Means the same as *limited partnership*.

limited partnership. A legal business organization that allows partners protection from liability up to the amount they have invested.

line of credit. The amount a person or corporation can purchase without putting up cash. Similar to a credit limit on a credit card.

M

marketing. The strategy behind the advertising, promotion, and sale of a service or product.

marketing plan. The blue print or road map of a business's advertising, promotion, and sales activities.

market survey. A research tool in which a business asks potential buyers what they want.

marks. The legal term used to describe any device a business uses to distinguish its products or services from those of others. A mark can be any word, name, brand, symbol, or logo.

mediation. An intervention by a professional third party to resolve a dispute.

mission. The purpose of a business.

multitasking. Doing more than one thing at a time.

N

networking. Your system for developing business contacts for advice, information, and support.

nonprofit corporation. A specific way of organizing a business for charitable or benevolent purposes.

P

portable business. A business that can be run in many different places.

product. Manufactured goods, merchandise, or inventions.

professional business. Business for a professionally licensed person, such as an attorney, CPA, or insurance agent.

professional corporation. A legal business organization recognized by some states for certain professionals such as attorneys, accountants, and insurance agents.

R

refund policy. A predetermined business policy that governs taking back merchandise that is defective, flawed, or unwanted by consumers.

S

S corporation. Specific business structure with rules set up by each state.

sales. The proceeds from the transfer of your product or service into the hands of a consumer.

sales tax. A tax imposed on the sale of goods and services. It is usually measured as a percentage of the retail price. Many states levy this type of tax.

self-insured. Not purchasing an insurance policy for known perils. Being prepared to pay the cost of events that are normally insured against such as fire, flood, weather destruction, inventory loss, etc.

service business. A business that sells services not a product, for example, a dry cleaner.

Social Security number (SSN). Can be used to pay your business taxes if the IRS does not require you to have an EIN.

sole proprietor. The only owner of a business and usually the only worker in it.

stamps.com. Software program for purchasing postage and tracking packages.

state registration. In accordance with state laws, the requirement that certain items or business be listed with the states where they reside. An example is your car that is registered in your state.

T

tax year. Twelve consecutive months in which a business calculates its taxable income and files its income tax return.

trade name. Name of a business that is something other than the full name of each of the owners.

trade secrets. Anything a business wants to keep confidential, such as lists of customers and recipes.

Truth in Lending Act. Law enacted to provide information for consumers who are requesting credit.

U

use tax. A tax paid in place of a sales tax.

W

withholding taxes. Amount of money your business withholds from your employees' wages for their income, Social Security, and Medicare obligations.

Z

zoning regulations. Laws governing the use of real property.

Appendix:
Secretary of State
Contact Information

The Secretary of State's Office in each state can:

- give you the current information about forms you need to file to start a business entity in that state and
- give you the site to their homepage, if they have one. You can go to it to choose and download forms.

NOTE: *Secretary of State's Office marked with 4-stars (****) are those that provide information applicable to all states.*

Alabama
Secretary of State
State Capital Building
600 Dexter Avenue
Montgomery, AL 36103
334-242-7205
www.sos.state.al.us

Alaska
Lieutenant Governor
P.O. Box 110001
Juneau, AK 99811-0001
907-465-3500
FAX 907-465-3532
www.state.ak.us

Arizona
Secretary of State
State Capitol
1700 West Washington
7th Floor
Phoenix, AZ 85007-2888
602-542-4285
FAX 602-542-1575
www.azsos.gov

Arkansas
Secretary of State
State Capitol
Room 256
Little Rock, AR 72201
501-682-1010
www.sos.arkansas.gov

California ****
Secretary of State
1500 11th Street
Sacramento, CA 95814
916-653-6814
www.ss.ca.gov

Colorado
Secretary of State
Suite 200
1700 Broadway
Denver, CO 80290
303-894-2200
FAX 303-869-4860
www.sos.state.co.us

Connecticut ****

Secretary of State
210 Capitol Avenue
Suite 104
Hartford, CT 06106
860-509-6200
FAX 860-509-6209
www.sots.state.ct.us

Delaware

Secretary of State
401 Federal Street
Suite 3
Dover, DE 19901
302-739-4111
FAX 302-739-3811
www.state.de.us/sos

District of Columbia

Secretary of the District
1350 Pennsylvania Avenue N.W.
Washington, DC 20004
202-727-6306
www.dc.gov

Florida

Secretary of State
R.A. Gray Building
500 South Bronough
Tallahassee, FL 32399
850-245-6500
www.dos.state.fl.us

Georgia ****

Secretary of State
214 State Capitol
Atlanta, GA 30334
404-656-2881
FAX 404-656-0513
www.sos.state.ga.us

Hawaii

Lieutenant Governor
State Capitol
Honolulu, HI 96813
808-586-0255
FAX 808-586-0231
www.hawaii.gov/ltgov

Idaho

Secretary of State
700 West Jefferson
Boise, ID 83720
208-334-2300
FAX 208-334-2282
www.idsos.state.id.us

Illinois ****

Secretary of State
213 State Capitol
Springfield, IL 62706
217-782-6961
www.sos.state.il.us
Also: www.commerce.state.il.us
or
www.illinoisbiz.biz/bus/sba.html

Indiana
Secretary of State
201 State House
Indianapolis, IN 46204
317-232-6531
FAX 317-233-3387
www.in.gov/sos

Iowa **
Secretary of State
Room 105
State Capitol
Des Moines, IA 50319
515-281-8993
FAX 515-242-5952
www.sos.state.ia.us

Kansas
Secretary of State
Memorial Hall
1st Floor
120 S.W. 10th Avenue
Topeka, KS 66612
785-296-4564
www.kssos.org/main.html

Kentucky **
Secretary of State
The Capitol Building
700 Capitol Avenue
Frankfort, KY 40601
502-564-3490
FAX 502-564-5687
http://sos.ky.gov
Also: www.ksbdc.org

Louisiana
Secretary of State
P.O. Box 94125
Baton Rouge, LA 70804
225-342-4479
FAX 225-342-0513
www.sec.state.la.us

Maine
Secretary of State
148 State House Station
Augusta, ME 04333
207-626-8400
FAX 207-287-8598
www.state.me.us/sos

Maryland
Secretary of State
State House
Annapolis, MD 21401
410-974-5521
www.sos.state.md.us

Massachusetts
Secretary of the Commonwealth
1 Ashburton Place
Room 1611
Boston, MA 02108
617-727-7030
FAX 617-742-4528
www.sec.state.ma.us

Michigan **
   Secretary of State
   Lansing, MI 48918
   517-322-1460
   www.michigan.gov/sos

Minnesota
   Secretary of State
   180 State Office Building
   100 Rev. Dr. Martin Luther King
      Jr. Boulevard
   St. Paul, MN 55155
   651-296-2803
   FAX 651-297-7067
   www.sos.state.mn.us

Mississippi
   Secretary of State
   P.O. Box 136
   Jackson, MS, 39205
   601-359-1350
   FAX 601-359-1499
   www.sos.state.ms.us

Missouri
   Secretary of State
   State Capitol
   Room 208
   Jefferson City, MO 65101
   573-751-4936
   FAX 573-751-2490
   www.sos.mo.gov

Montana **
   Secretary of State
   Room 260
   Capitol
   Helena, MT, 59620
   406-444-2034
   FAX 406-444-3976
   www.sos.state.mt.us/css/index.asp

Nebraska
   Secretary of State
   State Capitol
   Suite 2300
   Lincoln, NE 68509
   402-471-2554
   FAX 402-471-3237
   www.sos.state.ne.us

Nevada
   Secretary of State
   101 North Carson Street
   Suite 3
   Carson City, NV 89701
   775-684-5708
   FAX 775-684-5725
   www.sos.state.nv.us

New Hampshire
   Secretary of State
   State House
   Room 204
   Concord, NH 03301
   603-271-3242
   FAX 603-271-6316
   www.sos.nh.gov

New Jersey ****
Secretary of State
P.O. Box 300
Trenton, NJ 08625
609-984-1900
FAX 609-292-7665
www.state.nj.us/state

New Mexico
Secretary of State
State Capitol North Annex
Suite 300
Santa Fe, NM 87503
505-827-3600
FAX 505-827-3634
www.sos.state.nm.us

New York
Secretary of State
41 State Street
Albany, NY 12231
518-473-2492
FAX 518-474-1418
www.dos.state.ny.us/corp/
corpwww.html

North Carolina
Secretary of State
P.O. Box 29622
Raleigh, NC 27626-0622
919-807-2000
www.secstate.state.nc.us

North Dakota
Secretary of State
600 East Boulevard
Department 108
Bismarck, ND 58505-0500
701-328-2900
FAX 701-328-2992
www.state.nd.us/sec

Ohio
Secretary of State
180 East Broad Street
Columbus, OH 43215
614-466-2655
www.sos.state.oh.us/sos

Oklahoma
Secretary of State
2300 North Lincoln Boulevard
Suite 101
Oklahoma City, OK 73105-4897
405-521-3912
FAX 405-521-3771
www.sos.state.ok.us

Oregon ****
Secretary of State
136 State Capitol
Salem, OR 97310-0722
503-986-1523
FAX 503-986-1616
www.sos.state.or.us

Pennsylvania
Secretary of Commonwealth
North Office Building
Harrisburg, PA 17120
717-787-6458
FAX 717-787-1734
www.dos.state.pa.us

Rhode Island
Secretary of State
82 Smith Street
State House
Room 217
Providence, RI 02903
401-222-2357
FAX 401-222-1356
www.state.ri.us

South Carolina
Secretary of State
P.O. Box 11350
Columbia, SC 29211
803-734-2170
FAX 803-734-1661
www.scsos.com

South Dakota
Secretary of State
Capitol Building
500 East Capitol Avenue
Suite 204
Pierre, SD 57501-5070
605-773-3537
FAX 605-773-6580
www.sdsos.gov

Tennessee
Secretary of State
312 Eighth Avenue North
Nashville, TN 37243
615-741-2078
www.state.tn.us/sos

Texas
Secretary of State
P.O. Box 12887
Austin, TX 78711
512-463-5770
FAX 512-475-2761
www.sos.state.tx.us

Utah **
Lieutenant Governor
East Office Building
Suite E220
P.O. Box 142220
Salt Lake City, UT 84114-2220
801-538-1000
FAX 801-538-1528
www.utah.gov/ltgovernor

Vermont
Secretary of State
Redstone Building
26 Terrace Street
Drawer 09
Montpelier, VT 05609-1101
802-828-2363
FAX 802-828-2496
www.sec.state.vt.us

Virginia

Secretary of Commonwealth
Patrick Henry Building
4th Floor
1111 East Broad Street
Richmond, VA 23219
804-786-2441
www.soc.state.va.us

Washington

Secretary of State
Legislative Building
P.O. Box 40220
Olympia, WA 98504-0220
360-902-4151
www.secstate.wa.gov

West Virginia ****

Secretary of State
Building 1
Suite 157K
1900 Kanawha Boulevard East
Charleston, WV 253050-0770
304-558-8000
FAX 304-558-0900
www.wvsos.com/main.htm

Wisconsin

Secretary of State
30 West Mifflin Street
10th Floor
Madison, WI 53702
608-266-8888
FAX 608-266-3159
www.state.wi.us/agencies/sos

Wyoming

Secretary of State
State Capitol Building
Cheyenne, WY 82002
307-777-7378
FAX 307-777-6217
http://soswy.state.wy.us

Index